Sadlier
CHRIST IN US™

Parish Edition 5

"Christ In Us Grade 5 cover artwork speaks to the students' discovery of the challenges and opportunities of being missionary disciples to all of creation."

Reverend Donald Senior, C.P., S.T.D.

Sadlier Religion

This advanced publication copy has been printed prior to final publication and pending ecclesiastical approval.

Acknowledgments

This publication was printed with permission pending from the following copyright holders.

Excerpts from the *Catechism of the Catholic Church, second edition*, © 2000, Libreria Editrice Vaticana—United States Conference of Catholic Bishops, Washington, D.C. All rights reserved.

Scripture texts in this work are taken from the *New American Bible*, revised edition © 2010, 1991, 1986, 1970 Confraternity of Christian Doctrine, Washington, D.C. All Rights Reserved. No part of the *New American Bible* may be reproduced in any form without permission in writing from the copyright owner.

Excerpts from the English translation of *The Roman Missal* © 2010 International Commission on English in the Liturgy, Inc. (ICEL). All rights reserved.

Excerpts from the *Lectionary for Mass for Use in the Dioceses of the United States of America, second typical edition* © 2001, 1998, 1997, 1986, 1970 Confraternity of Christian Doctrine, Inc., Washington, D.C. All rights reserved. No portion of this text may be reproduced by any means without permission in writing from the copyright owner.

Quotations from papal addresses, audiences, homilies, speeches, messages, meditations, encyclicals, and other Vatican documents are from www.vatican.va and copyright © by Libreria Editrice Vaticana.

His Holiness Pope Francis, Twitter posts: September 9, 2013, 2:12 a.m., October 17, 2013, 6:45 a.m., and February 28, 2014, 3:28 a.m. http://twitter.com/Pontifex

Excerpt from "Issues and Action: Cultural Diversity—African American—Resources: The Gift of African American Sacred Song," United States Conference of Catholic Bishops, Inc., http://www.usccb.org/issues-and-action/cultural-diversity/african-american/resources/upload/The-Gift-of-African-American-Sacred-Song-Sr-Thea-Bowman.pdf

Excerpt from Thomas McNally, C.S.C., and William George Storey, D.M.S., Editors, *Day by Day: The Notre Dame Prayer Book for Students*, Ave Maria Press, Notre Dame, IN, 1975. Copyright © 1975 by Ave Maria Press.

"One Bread, One Body" © 2018 John Foley, S.J. Published by OCP, 5536 NE Hassalo, Portland, OR 97213. All rights reserved.

p. 24: *CCC*, 78: *DV* 8 § 1

p. 27: *Catechism of the Catholic Church*, 221: Cf. *1 Cor* 2:7–16; *Eph* 3:9–12

p. 63: *CCC*, 1099: Cf. *Jn* 14:26

p. 64: *CCC*, 1210: Cf. St. Thomas Aquinas, *STh* III, 65, 1

p. 112: *Catechism of the Catholic Church*, 1718: St. Thomas Aquinas, *Expos. in symb. apost.* I

p. 120: *Catechism of the Catholic Church*, 1966: St. Augustine, *De serm. Dom.* 1,1:PL 34,1229–1230

p. 171: *CCC*, 2652: *Jn* 4:14

William H. Sadlier, Inc.
9 Pine Street
New York, NY 10005-4700

ISBN: 978-0-8215-3695-7
123456789 WEBC 23 22 21 20 19

Christ In Us was developed in collaboration with the wisdom of the community. The team included respected catechetical, liturgical, pastoral, and theological experts who shared their insights and inspired its development.

With grateful acknowledgment of
William Sadlier Dinger and Frank Sadlier Dinger
for their leadership, vision, and commitment to excellence in the development
of Sadlier's catechetical programs and resources since 1963

Theological and Liturgical Consultants

Most Reverend Christopher James Coyne
Bishop of Burlington, VT

Donna Eschenauer, Ph.D.
Associate Dean, Associate Professor of
    Pastoral Theology
St. Joseph's Seminary and College

Rita Ferrone, M.Div.

Thomas Kendzia
Sadlier National Consultant for
    Liturgy and Music

Reverend Monsignor John Pollard, M. Ed. S.T.L.

Alissa Thorell, M.T.S

John B. Angotti, M.A.P.S.

Barbara Sutton, D.Min.

Kathleen Dorsey Bellow, D.Min.

Scripture Consultant

Reverend Donald Senior, C.P., S.T.D.
Chancellor and President Emeritus
    Catholic Theological Union

Catechetical Consultants

Amy Welborn, M.A.

Susan Stark

Sr. Theresa Engel, O.S.F.
Member of the School Sisters of St. Francis

Maureen A. Kelly, M.A.

Karla Manternach, M.A.

Woodeene Koenig-Bricker, M.A.

Connie Clark

Shannon Chisholm, Ph.D.

Susan M. Sink

Maureen Shaughnessy, S.C.

Lori Dahlhoff, Ed.D.

Andrea D. Chavez-Kopp, M.Ed.

Educational Consultants

Richard Culatta

Heidi Hayes Jacobs, Ed.D.

Jay McTighe

Allie Johnston

Learning Style Inclusion Consultants

Charleen Katra, M.A.

Jennifer Ochoa, M.Ed., LDT/C

Inculturation Consultants

Luis J. Medina
Director, Bilingual Catechesis

Charlene Howard, M.A.

Michael P. Howard, M.A.
Eat the Scroll Ministry

Catholic Social Teaching

Kristin Witte, D.Min.

Genevieve Jordan Laskey, M.A.

Michael Jordan Laskey, M.A.

Media and Technology Consultants

Spirit Juice Studios

Top Floor Productions

Sr. Caroline Cerveny, S.S.J.-T.O.S.F., D.Min.

Reviewers and Contributors

Jennifer Hayhurst

Concetta M. Duval, Ed.D.

Trenton W. Mattingly, M.A.

Debi Mahr, M.A.

Mary Homola, M.A.

Linda Mele Dougherty, M.A.

Mary Jane Krebbs, Ph.D.

Darcy Osby, M.Div.

Hugh M. Keenan

Sadlier Consultant Team

Steven Botsford
Senior Director of Digital Catechesis

Suzan Larroquette, M.T.S.
Senior Director of Catechetical Consultant Services

Kathleen Hendricks, M.A.
National Catechetical Consultant Contributing Writer

John Collins, M.Ed.
National Religion Consultant

Writing/Development Team

Diane Lampitt, M.Ed.
Vice President, Product Manager, Religion

Blake Bergen
Vice President, Religion Editorial

Deacon Matthew Halbach, Ph.D.
Senior Director of Catechesis

Regina Kelly, M.A.
Editorial Director, Religion

Gloria Shahin, M.A.
Senior Editorial Director, Religion

Mary Carol Kendzia, M.S.
Research and Development Director, Religion

Robert Vigneri, M.S.
Executive Editor, Religion

Editorial Staff
Tina Dennelly, Linda Nicholson,
Roger Ochoa, Amanda Pisciotta

Publishing Operations Team

Patricia Coryell
Senior Vice President & Publisher

Kevin Feyen
Vice President, Shared Services

Carole Uettwiller
Vice President, Supply Chain

Vince Gallo
Senior Creative Director

Francesca O'Malley
Art/Design Director

Cesar Llacuna
Senior Image Manager

Roderick Gammon
Senior Director, Digital Strategy

Toby Carson
Digital Design Director

Cheryl Golding
Senior Production Director

Laura Reischour
Project Manager

Evie Alvarez
Program Manager

Jovito Pagkalinawan
Electronic Prepress Director

Yolanda Miley
Image Rights & Permissions Director

Lucy Rotondi
Business Manager

Design/Image Staff
Kevin Butler, Nancy Figueiredo, Stephen Flanagan,
Debrah Kaiser, Gabriel Ricci, Bob Schatz,
Daniel Sherman

Production Staff
Robin D'Amato, Carol Lin, Vincent McDonough,
Allison Pagkalinawan, Brad Tucker

Contents

Prayer: Meditation

Psalm 105:3

• God is truth and love. • We come to know God most fully through Sacred Scripture. • We come to know God through Jesus. • The Church passes on all that she holds true through Scripture, Tradition, and the sacraments.

Lesson Test: Show What You Know

Partners in Faith: Saint Ignatius of Loyola

Mini-Task: How can I show God to others?

At Home: Remember experiences of God's love.

Prayer: Praise

Catechism of the Catholic Church, **221**

• God can be known through creation. • The Blessed Trinity is a mystery of faith, in which God is revealed as Father, Son, and Holy Spirit. • In the sacraments, we share in the life of the Trinity. • The Church is a sacrament that reveals the Trinity to God's people.

Glory Be

Lesson Test: Show What You Know

Partners in Faith: Juan de Zumárraga

Mini-Task: How do I live out my belief in God?

At Home: Show respect for all life.

Prayer: Petition

Roman Missal, **Eucharistic Prayer IV, 117**

Psalm 8:6

• God created us with a body and soul. • The Church supports and nourishes our faith. • God created Adam and Eve to live in friendship with him. • Everyone who dies in God's friendship will have the joy of eternal life with him.

Lesson Test: Show What You Know

Partners in Faith: Saint Peter

Mini-Task: How can I grow in holiness?

At Home: Strengthen one another's faith.

Prayer: *Lectio* and *Visio Divina*

Pope Francis, *Angelus*

• The Holy Spirit prepared Mary for her work as the Mother of God. • The Incarnation is the mystery that Jesus, the only Son of God, became human. • Jesus is the Savior who came into the world to save us from sin. • At the Ascension, the Risen Christ was taken up into heaven.

Lesson Test: Show What You Know

Partners in Faith: Saint Catherine Labouré

Mini-Task: How do I come to know Mary, the Mother of God?

At Home: Pray for family members who have died.

Prayer: Intercession

Rite of Baptism for Children

1 Peter 2:9

• In Baptism, we become members of the Church. • The People of God are the temple of the Holy Spirit and the sacrament of Christ. • The Church is divinely established, motivated by love, and guided by the Holy Spirit. • Through our Baptism, we continue Jesus' work in the Church today.

Apostles' Creed

Lesson Test: Show What You Know

Partners in Faith: Blessed Sára Salkaházi

Mini-Task: How does my parish reflect the work of the Church?

At Home: Discuss stories of family Baptisms.

Your Spiritual Journey

Christ In Us offers a saint for every grade. As you journey through each unit, remember to pray to your grade's saint. Ask him or her to help guide you to be closer to Jesus Christ.

Saint Ignatius of Loyola was born in the Basque country of Spain in 1491 and was the youngest of thirteen children. Ignatius' mother died soon after his birth.

In his youth, Ignatius developed a passion for military life and enjoyed dressing up as a soldier. He joined the army at the age of 17.

Ignatius was a fearless soldier and participated in many battles without injury. His bravery and leadership were recognized by the royal family of his region, and he soon became an important leader.

But Ignatius' streak of good fortune came to an end in 1521, when he was seriously hurt at the Battle of Pamplona. He was hit by a cannonball, injuring his legs. He would limp for the rest of his life. The military career in which Ignatius took so much pride had come to an end.

The injury, however, set the stage for a religious conversion. During the time his legs were healing, Ignatius read Scripture and books about the lives of saints.

In 1522 Ignatius traveled to a monastery, where he confessed his sins. He placed his sword at the altar of the Virgin Mary as a sign that he would now be a soldier for Jesus Christ.

At the age of 48, Ignatius formed the Society of Jesus. It is a religious order better known as the Jesuits. Ignatius wanted the Jesuits to travel around the world as missionaries. He wanted to spread the Gospel of Jesus Christ by establishing schools, colleges, and seminaries.

How can you be a missionary for Christ?

Welcome to **Christ In Us**, an exciting way to grow in your Catholic faith!

Each one of us is on a journey to love and know Jesus Christ. Imagine if every person who met you knew you were a friend of Christ!

Together in this program

we will **ENCOUNTER** Jesus Christ

we will **ACCOMPANY** him in our lives

we will **WITNESS** to our faith.

You will use this book as well as your online digital portal as you discover and grow closer to Jesus Christ.

As you journey in your faith, you can think about these questions:

"Examine me, Lord, and test me; search my heart and mind.

Your mercy is before my eyes; I walk guided by your faithfulness."

Psalm 26: 2–3

Why is it important to have Christ live in you?

What would happen if you did not have Jesus in your life?

How does your faith, the Church, and your family help bring you closer to God?

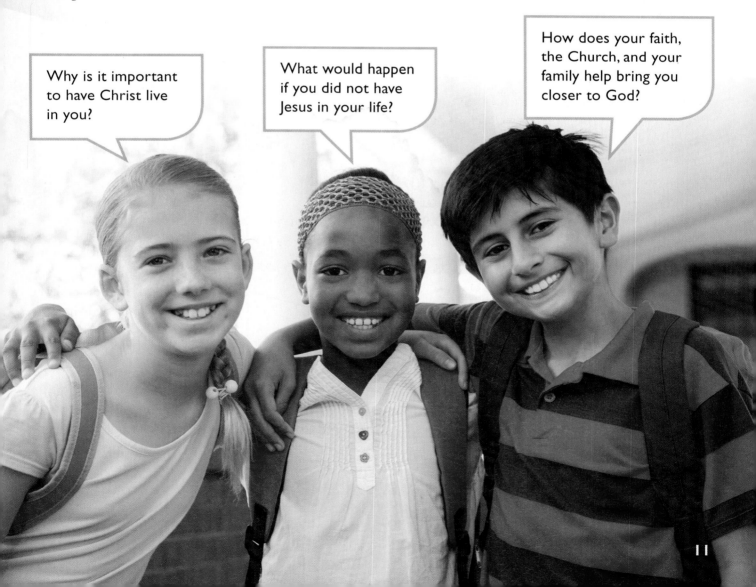

Every lesson has four **Spiraling Main Ideas**.
Here is an example.

Each lesson has one or more **Faith Words** to help you understand the important words we use as Catholics.

We come to know God through Sacred Scripture.

God reveals himself to us in ways we can understand. One of these ways is through human words. **Sacred Scripture** is God's revelation in human words. In Sacred Scripture, God speaks to his children. He lovingly meets us and talks with us. Sacred Scripture is God's Word to us and for us. God is the author of Sacred Scripture. He inspired human writers to faithfully communicate the truth about who he is. The Holy Spirit guided the minds, hearts, and hands of the human authors of Scripture to write the saving truth about God.

Sacred Scripture is contained in the books of the Old Testament and New Testament in the Bible. Scripture tells the story of God's love for his people and their response to his love. When we read or listen to Scripture, the same Holy Spirit who inspired the writers of Scripture helps us understand God's plan for us. In the words of Sacred Scripture, we encounter the Incarnate Word of God: Jesus Christ.

Faith Word

Sacred Scripture
see p. 259

Be sure to look at all the wonderful photos and beautiful art found in the pages of your book.

Activity

Below are some names for God found in Sacred Scripture. Using your Bible and/or dictionary, describe what these names mean.

Which of these is your favorite name for God? Why? Share with a friend.

Abba	Messiah
Advocate	Paraclete
Christ	Son of Man
Counselor	Son of God
Creator	Spirit of Truth
Intercessor	Witness
Lamb of God	Yahweh
Lord	

22 ACCOMPANY

As you explore this question, you might be asked to stop and think more about it and then do a short **Activity** to answer it better.

You will be asked to **Show What You Know** by writing down the answers to some short questions pertaining to the lesson.

You will not be alone as you journey through **Christ In Us**. You will have lots of **Partners in Faith**—saints and other holy people who lived amazing lives—walking with you.

Along with Saint Ignatius, here are some other Partners in Faith whom you will meet throughout the book!

Saint Thomas More

Saint Peter

Saint Catherine Labouré

Sister Rose Hawthorne

Blessed Sára Salkaházi

Saint Andrew Kim Taegŏn

Saint Rose of Lima

Saint Anselm

Next, you will be asked to go to your **Portfolio** to creatively share how you can bring Christ to the world.

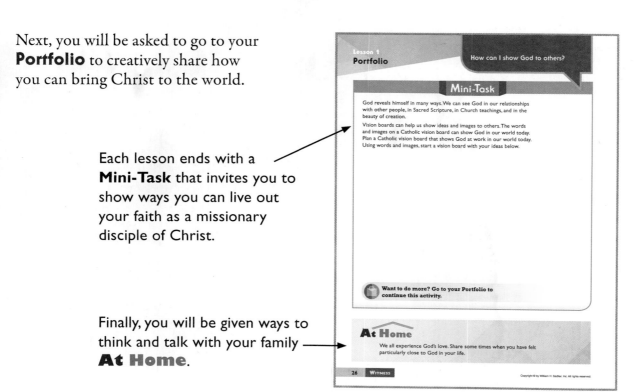

Each lesson ends with a **Mini-Task** that invites you to show ways you can live out your faith as a missionary disciple of Christ.

Finally, you will be given ways to think and talk with your family **At Home**.

Christ In Us features an online portal filled with exciting media and activities to go with the lessons in your book. If you see one of these icons below in your book, you know it's time to visit the student portal for more. (Note: Not every icon will appear in your book.)

 Participate in lesson prayers, whose words are online and downloadable.

Learn more about the lesson's **Did You Know?** topic by watching an interesting video and doing an activity.

 Learn more about the lesson's **Partner in Faith** by watching an online video and completing the activity that follows.

Listen to Scripture verses and Catholic prayers and learn them by heart.

Find fun activities to share and recall what you have learned.

Show What You Know by completing online assessments.

Read and remember the **Faith Words** definitions.

Complete projects and tasks in the online **Portfolio** or *Portfolio Workbook*.

Listen to the songs for your grade level and sing along!

Your Songs for Grade 5

Unit Songs	Liturgical Catechesis Seasonal Songs
Unit 1: "We Have Been Told," David Haas	**Lent:** "Your Grace Is Enough," Matt Maher
Unit 2: "Light of Christ," Tom Kendzia	**The Church Year:** "The Lord Has Done Great Things For Us," Jamie Cortez
Unit 3: "I Send You Out," John Angotti	**Ordinary Time:** "We Are His People," Greg Walton
Unit 4: "Here I Am, Lord," Dan Schutte	**Triduum:** "I Will Have Faith In You," Sarah Hart
Unit 5: "We Are Called," David Haas	

Your journey continues with your login to *Christ In Us* Digital!

Here you can explore all the exciting resources that blend together with your textbook.

Take a look at your personalized online dashboard. Everything you need is at your fingertips!

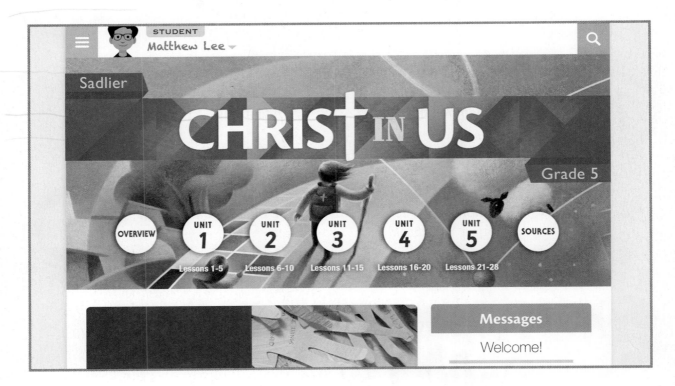

- Think of your portfolio as your digital backpack! Here you can get your assignments, see reminders, send emails, and even talk to your catechist.

- Interactive Mini-Tasks! Here you will be able to share exciting activities with others. You will be able to get hands on and creative by making videos or interactive posters.

- Listen with your heart and pray the prayers of *Lectio* and *Visio Divina*, praise, petition, intercession, litany, meditation, blessing, and thanksgiving from your lesson.

- Track your progress with digital quizzes and tests.

Have a wonderful year!

Unit 1
The Faith Professed

The Nativity

Unit Prayer

Leader: Saint Ignatius of Loyola prayed: "Give me only your love and your grace; that is enough for me." Through the sacraments, we discover God's love and grace.

Let us listen to how the sacraments have changed the lives of people among us.

Listen to the stories of missionary disciples among us.

Leader: Let us pray: Jesus, we receive your love and grace in the sacraments and through the stories we shared today. In thanksgiving for the gift of the sacraments in our lives, we pray:

Leader: O God, at Baptism we are clothed in your love and sent to be a living sign of Christ.

All: Give me only your love and your grace; that is enough for me.

Leader: When you forgive our sins, we celebrate your unconditional love for us.

All: Give me only your love and your grace; that is enough for me.

Leader: In the Eucharist you nourish us with your Body and Blood, filling us with your presence.

All: Give me only your love and your grace; that is enough for me.

Leader: With Saint Ignatius we say: "Give me only your love and your grace; that is enough for me."

All: Give me only your love and your grace; that is enough for me.

End the Unit Prayer by singing the song for this unit.

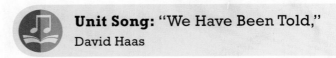

Unit Song: "We Have Been Told," David Haas

Missionary Discipleship

How have you been a living sign of Christ with your family and friends? What happened? How did you feel? What are the ways that you are nourished with the Body and Blood of Christ in the Eucharist?

How do we know God?

God has planted in every human heart the desire to know him. God reveals himself to us so that we can share in his life and love. We come to know who God is when we read and listen to Sacred Scripture. We know God when we celebrate and take part in the holy sacrifice of the Mass. God reveals himself to us through Sacred Scripture and in Sacred Tradition. He reveals himself to us most fully in his Son, Jesus.

Go to the digital portal for a meditation prayer.

"Glory in his holy name;
let hearts that seek the Lord rejoice!"

Psalm 105:3

God is truth and love.

God created us out of love. He gave each of us the desire to know our purpose in life and to discover life's truth and meaning. God never stops calling us to be close to him.

We can never know everything about God or completely understand his plan. God is a **mystery**, which means that he is greater than the human mind's ability to understand. Words alone cannot fully describe who God is. Over time, however, God gradually revealed himself. It is Jesus Christ who fully reveals God to us. He is true God and true man, as we profess in the Creed at Mass. **Divine Revelation** is God's making himself known to us. Through Divine Revelation, we come to know his plan of salvation for all people.

God is the truth that all people seek. God is the love for which all people long. The *Catechism of the Catholic Church* teaches that "God's very being is Truth and Love" (*CCC*, 231).

Faith Words

mystery see p. 258

Divine Revelation see p. 257

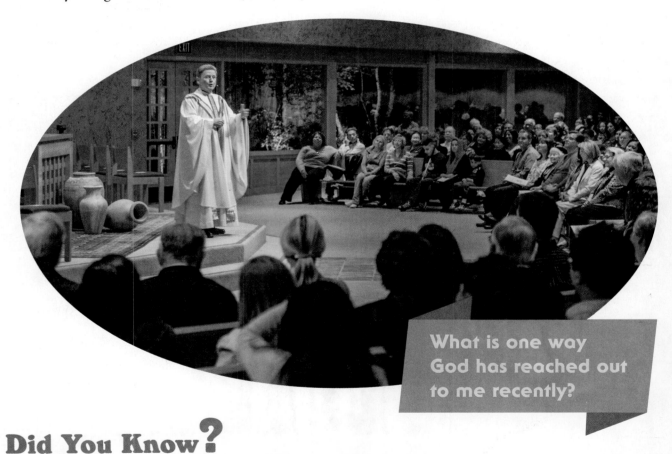

What is one way God has reached out to me recently?

Did You Know?

The Bible uses different styles of writing.

God's creation reveals his truth, love, beauty, and goodness. All of creation gives praise and honor to him. We discover that God's love is without limits. Even though the first man and woman turned away from him, God did not end his relationship with humanity. God's covenant with Noah, Abraham, and others shows us that he has never stopped reaching out to us with his saving love.

One way we come to know God is through one another. We are all created in God's image and likeness, so we can see God in each other and in our relationships with others.

One Church, Many Cultures

Knowing that we are all made in God's image and likeness can help us understand that we are meant to respect and show kindness to all people. There are people in our communities who may be different from us, but we are all equal in God's eyes. The fact that we are made in God's image, despite our differences, reminds us that God is a mystery we can never fully understand. The Church teaches that we can see God's love and care in everyone.

Activity

Name two people who have helped you come to know God. Write a short prayer thanking God for those people in your life.

My mom and Dad help me learn about god. and i pray every night but, sometimes i forget. It is god to pray, and my mom is a nuse, my dad is a ingerner,

We come to know God through Sacred Scripture.

God reveals himself to us in ways we can understand. One of these ways is through human words. **Sacred Scripture** is God's revelation in human words. In Sacred Scripture, God speaks to his children. He lovingly meets us and talks with us. Sacred Scripture is God's Word to us and for us. God is the author of Sacred Scripture. He inspired human writers to faithfully communicate the truth about who he is. The Holy Spirit guided the minds, hearts, and hands of the human authors of Scripture to write the saving truth about God.

Sacred Scripture is contained in the books of the Old Testament and New Testament in the Bible. Scripture tells the story of God's love for his people and their response to his love. When we read or listen to Scripture, the same Holy Spirit who inspired the writers of Scripture helps us understand God's plan for us. In the words of Sacred Scripture, we encounter the Incarnate Word of God: Jesus Christ.

Faith Word

Sacred Scripture
see p. 259

Activity

Below are some names for God found in Sacred Scripture. Using your Bible and/or dictionary, describe what these names mean.

Which of these is your favorite name for God? Why? Share with a friend.

Abba	Messiah
Advocate	Paraclete
Christ	Son of Man
Counselor	Son of God
Creator	Spirit of Truth
Intercessor	Witness
Lamb of God	Yahweh
Lord	

We come to know God most fully through Jesus.

"For God so loved the world that he gave his only Son, so that everyone who believes in him might not perish but might have eternal life" (John 3:16).

This Scripture verse reveals a central truth of Christian faith. God sent his own Son to live among us and to save us. God the Father's love for us is beyond anything we can imagine.

God has never stopped loving us. Even when his people turned away from him, God remained true to his covenant. Jesus Christ is the New Covenant. God fully revealed who he is in Jesus, in whom he has established his covenant forever. God is always faithful, always loving, and always calling us back to himself.

Jesus tells us: "I am the way and the truth and the life. No one comes to the Father except through me" (John 14:6). We read about the life of Christ in the four Gospels, which begin the New Testament.

The Gospel writers wanted to share their faith with others. They wanted to share the truth revealed to them by Jesus: "Whoever has seen me has seen the Father" (John 14:9). At the heart of the Gospels is the revelation that "Jesus is the Messiah, the Son of God" (John 20:31).

Every single thing about Jesus' life reveals who God is. Jesus, the Word of God, is the fulfillment of Divine Revelation.

The Scribe Stood to Tempt Jesus by James Tissot

The Church passes on all that she holds true through Scripture, Tradition, and the sacraments.

Faith Word

Sacred Tradition see p. 259

The Church, with the help of the Holy Spirit, guides and teaches us the truth about who God is. At Mass, we read and listen to Sacred Scripture. In the Eucharist, God reveals the depth of his love for us. For in the Eucharist, Christ offers his sacrifice of praise and thanksgiving to his Father. We share in the grace of salvation.

The revelation of the Good News of Jesus Christ as lived out in the Church, past and present, is called **Sacred Tradition**. Sacred Tradition is separate from, but closely connected to, Sacred Scripture. Together Sacred Scripture and Sacred Tradition ensure that the authentic revelation of God is passed down to all generations. They shape our faith in Jesus Christ and our life as his disciples.

We especially encounter the Good News of God's love in the Seven Sacraments, which Jesus gave to his Church. Through Sacred Tradition, the Church passes on "to every generation all that she . . . is, [and] all that she believes" (*CCC*, 78). In this way, the knowledge of God reaches the ends of the earth.

What Makes Us Catholic?

The things your family does regularly are called family traditions. The word *tradition* spelled with a small "t" means "customs." *Tradition* with a capital "T," on the other hand, refers to the authority, words, and deeds of Jesus passed down to his Apostles and their successors, the bishops. The celebration of the sacraments and the official teachings of the Church are examples of big *T* Tradition, also called Sacred Tradition.

Partners in Faith

Saint Ignatius of Loyola

Saint Ignatius was a Spanish soldier. He was badly hurt when he was hit by a cannonball. While he was recovering, he read about Jesus and the saints. Eventually he founded the religious order called the Jesuits. He helped people know God with his book called *Spiritual Exercises*. Saint Ignatius wrote prayers and reflections that we still use. The first Jesuit to be pope was Pope Francis.

 Learn more about the life of Saint Ignatius of Loyola.

Faith Words

mystery **Divine Revelation**
Sacred Scripture **Sacred Tradition**

 ## Show What You Know

Match the terms to the correct definitions.

1. Sacred Scripture

2. Divine Revelation

3. mystery

4. Sacred Tradition

something that is beyond our ability to understand completely

the revelation of the Good News of Jesus Christ as lived out in the Church, past and present

holy writings in which God speaks to us in human words

the way God makes himself known to us

Live Your Faith

• How can you come to know more about God?

_____

_____

_____

_____

_____

_____

_____

_____

• How can you treat others to show them that they are made in God's image and likeness?

_____

_____

_____

_____

_____

_____

_____

_____

Mini-Task

God reveals himself in many ways. We can see God in our relationships with other people, in Sacred Scripture, in Church teachings, and in the beauty of creation.

Vision boards can help us show ideas and images to others. The words and images on a Catholic vision board can show God in our world today. Plan a Catholic vision board that shows God at work in our world today. Using words and images, start a vision board with your ideas below.

Want to do more? Go to your Portfolio to continue this activity.

At Home

We all experience God's love. Share some times when you have felt particularly close to God in your life.

Who is God?

From the beginning of time, people have searched to know who God is. We can know God through his creation. Creation points back to God, the Creator. But to help us know him more fully, God revealed himself to us in Sacred Scripture. He revealed himself to be Father, Son, and Holy Spirit. God also reveals himself in the teachings and the life of the Church, particularly the sacraments. God reveals himself most fully through his Son, Jesus Christ.

Go to the digital portal for a prayer of praise.

"God's very being is love. By sending his only Son and the Spirit of Love in the fullness of time, God has revealed his innermost secret: God himself is an eternal exchange of love, Father, Son, and Holy Spirit, and he has destined us to share in that exchange."

Catechism of the Catholic Church, 221

Faith Word

sanctified see p. 259

God can be known through creation.

God knows that the deepest desire of the human heart is to seek and find him. In his goodness, God has given us ways of coming to know him. One amazing way is through creation. Creation was God's first witness to us of his almighty love and wisdom. In creation, God took the first step toward us. Freely and without any help, God laid the foundation of his loving goodness.

God created us to be open to truth and beauty. When we use this gift of openness, we can look at God's creation and see all that it has to teach us about who God is. A sunset on an autumn horizon might leave us amazed by its beauty. From this experience, we know that God is beauty. When we witness the miracle of new life, such as when a baby bird hatches from its egg or a butterfly emerges from its cocoon, we know that God is life-giving.

The high point of God's act of creation was the creation of man and woman. God created man and woman in his image and likeness. He created us to know what is good and right, and with a longing for happiness. God gave us freedom and a conscience and the ability to reason. We can use these gifts to know that God exists.

The Church uses the gifts of creation in her celebration of the sacraments. These gifts, such as water, oil, bread, and wine, are **sanctified**, or made holy, in the sacraments. By their use in the sacraments, these gifts of creation become sacred. They become physical signs that point to the invisible grace of God. In the sacraments, we encounter Jesus and receive God's grace.

Activity

Think about something that has amazed you about God's creation. What is it? Write about it and why it amazed you. Share your thoughts with a partner or with the group.

Did You Know?

There are many ways to bless with holy water.

The Blessed Trinity is a mystery of faith, in which God is revealed as Father, Son, and Holy Spirit.

"In the name of the Father, and of the Son, and of the Holy Spirit. Amen." With water and these words, we are baptized into the faith of the Church. These words and the Sign of the Cross marked on the forehead of those celebrating the Sacrament of Baptism signify the central mystery of the Christian faith: the mystery of the Blessed Trinity. Whenever we pray the Sign of the Cross, we profess an essential belief of the Church.

Through Divine Revelation, God revealed himself as Father, Son, and Holy Spirit. God is the Father, the Trinity's first Person and first principle, and the origin of all creation. Together with the creative action of the eternal Word (the Son) and his Wisdom (the Holy Spirit), God the Father is the Creator, the author of life. Creation is a work of the Blessed Trinity.

The Church teaches these truths about the Blessed Trinity:

- The Trinity is One God in Three Persons: Father, Son, and Holy Spirit. Each Person of the Trinity is God.

- God the Father, God the Son, and God the Holy Spirit are distinct from one another. They are not different ways of being God. They are three identifiable Persons.

 Glory Be

- Father, Son, and Holy Spirit are in a relationship of perfect unity and love. They are inseparable in what they are and in what they do.

The Blessed Trinity is always present in the Church. Most especially, the Trinity is at work in the sacraments where we share in God's life. In the sacraments, we encounter Jesus. The Gift of the Holy Spirit draws us closer to Christ.

What Makes Us Catholic?

The Blessed Trinity is the central truth of our faith. In the fourth century A.D., the Nicene Creed affirmed that the Holy Spirit "proceeds from the Father and the Son," not just from the Father. This change helped the Church better understand that the Blessed Trinity is One God in Three Persons. We understand that Saint Patrick used the three leaves of a shamrock to explain the Blessed Trinity to his listeners. Today, we can use others symbols to help us understand the Blessed Trinity, such as the Trinity Knot, a triangle, or the *fleur-de-lis*. Which symbol would help you explain the Blessed Trinity?

In the sacraments, we share in the life of the Blessed Trinity.

Think about your best friend's name. What thoughts come to mind when you say it aloud? Just as when you think of your relationship with your friend, you see that person's face in your mind or hear his or her voice. Your friend's name, which is a series of letters, becomes more important than the word itself. Names are like that. They are much more than what they appear to be, particularly when we know the person.

What thoughts come to mind when you say the name *Jesus*? In the Bible, names often took on importance beyond the actual word. They often described a role a person played in God's plan of salvation.

The name *Jesus* means "God saves." Jesus, in whom God fully reveals himself, is the fulfillment of God's plan of salvation. In order for us to participate fully in God's life, Jesus gave the Church the sacraments. The Holy Spirit makes present the mystery of Christ. Every time we gather for the liturgy, the Holy Spirit brings us into communion with Christ (see *Catechism of the Catholic Church*, 1108). The sacraments, through the power of the Holy Spirit, make Jesus' saving work present. Through the sacraments, we share in the life of the Blessed Trinity.

The Church shares her beliefs through Scripture, Tradition, and the sacraments.

From the beginning of time, the Holy Spirit had been preparing his people for the coming of the Messiah. Jesus began his ministry by proclaiming: "The Spirit of the Lord is upon me" (Luke 4:18). These words were originally spoken by the prophet Isaiah. When Jesus proclaimed them in a synagogue, they meant something important to the people who were gathered in the synagogue listening to Jesus. Through these words, Jesus revealed that his mission and the mission of the Holy Spirit were the same.

The relationship between Jesus and the Holy Spirit is so close that, before he died, Jesus promised his disciples that he would send the Holy Spirit upon them. The Spirit would be their helper. He would reveal the truth about God to the disciples.

Then Jesus gave the disciples these instructions: "Go, therefore, and make disciples of all nations, baptizing them in the name of the Father, and of the Son, and of the holy Spirit, teaching them to observe all that I have commanded you. And behold, I am with you always, until the end of the age" (Matthew 28:19–20). At that moment, the mission of Christ and the Spirit became the mission of the Church.

One Church, Many Cultures

The Church's mission to "make disciples of all nations" does not mean that Catholics should force people everywhere to accept our faith. God invites people to share in his love. He does not force them. Catholic missionaries share God's Word all over the world. We do the same in our own communities. In fact, the Church tells us that we are all called to be "missionary disciples." God wants us to show our faith by the way we live so that people will see his goodness in everything we say and do.

Saint Teresa of Calcutta founded the the Missionaries of Charity to help the poor, the sick, and the disabled. Here they carry out their mission in Brazil.

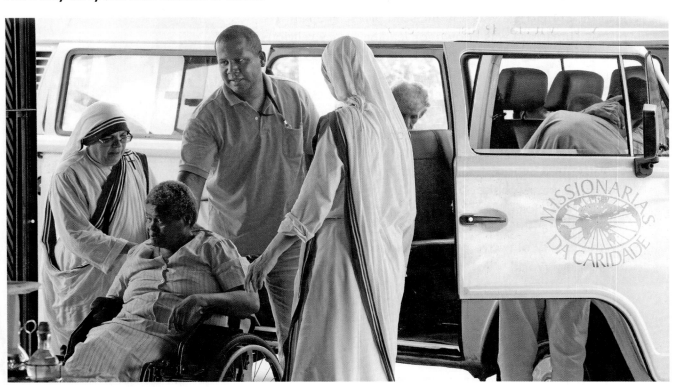

Jesus, more than anyone or anything else, helps us see God's presence in the world. Through the sacraments, we encounter Jesus and receive his grace. The Church is a sign of the unity of the Blessed Trinity and all people. The Church is Christ's instrument for the salvation of all people.

The Holy Spirit works in the Church to bring her members to Christ and to show us who Christ is. The Spirit opens our minds and hearts to the mystery of Christ's saving love. The Holy Spirit makes present the mystery of the Blessed Trinity through the sacraments. We are drawn into communion with God, especially in the Eucharist. The Spirit is always at work in the Church, building her up, bringing her life, and sanctifying her, or making her holy.

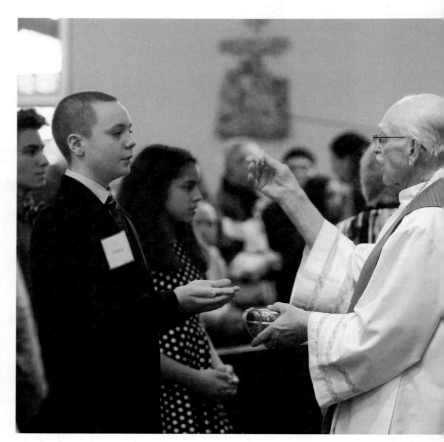

Partners in Faith

Juan de Zumárraga

Juan de Zumárraga was a Franciscan priest in Spain. As a priest, Zumárraga was known for leading a very religious, poor, and humble life. With the Spanish king's help, Zumárraga became the first bishop of Mexico in 1530. He was given the title "Protector of the Indians." Zumárraga believed his role was to make sure natives in New Spain were not treated poorly. Under his spiritual leadership, he fought for the rights of the people and built the first school, hospital, and printing press in Mexico. It was Archbishop Zumárraga who received Saint Juan Diego's cloak with the miraculous image of the Virgin of Guadalupe on December 12, 1531. Zumárraga's fight for the dignity of native peoples helped grow the Church in the New World.

 Learn more about the life of Juan de Zumárraga.

Faith Word

sanctified

Show What You Know

Complete the sentences.

1. When something is made holy, we say that it is _____.

2. Water, oil, bread, and wine are made holy in the _____.

3. The Blessed Trinity is a _____ of faith.

4. The _____ is a sacrament that reveals the
   Blessed Trinity to God's people.

Live Your Faith

• What is a way you can describe the Blessed Trinity to a friend who does not
  know God?

_____

_____

_____

_____

_____

_____

_____

_____

_____

• In what way can spending time in God's creation help you know him better?

_____

_____

_____

_____

_____

_____

_____

_____

How do I live out my belief in God?

Mini-Task

We are created in the image and likeness of God. And just as the Persons of the Blessed Trinity—Father, Son, and Holy Spirit—relate to each other in unconditional love, so we are called to love our friends and family.

Bio-poems tell about a person in a special way, using seven lines that describe the person. On the lines below, write a bio-poem about someone with whom you have a close relationship.

First Name:

Friend of:

Son/Daughter of:

Student at:

Working on:

Grateful for:

Last Name:

 Want to do more? Go to your Portfolio to continue this activity.

God gives us life. We are called to honor his gift of life. Choose one way your family can show respect for all life.

Why did God make us?

God created us to share in his life and love forever. God created us with a body and a soul to experience his presence and the wonders of the created world. Through the gift of faith, supported and nurtured through our families and through the Church and the sacraments, we come to know God's plan of holiness and justice. We see the gift of God's grace active in our lives. We grow in holiness, and we look forward to eternal life and friendship with God.

Go to the digital portal for a prayer of petition.

*"We give you praise, Father most holy,
for you are great
and you have fashioned all your works
in wisdom and in love."*

Roman Missal, Eucharistic Prayer IV, 117

Faith Word

soul see p. 259

What is something I have felt deep in my soul?

God created us with a body and soul.

God created the universe and everything in it from nothing. The greatest of all God's works is the human person. Through their intellect and will, humans are able to know and love God.

The writer of the Psalms described it this way:

"You have made [them] little less than a god, crowned [them] with glory and honor" (Psalm 8:6).

God created us to share in his own life. How does this great mystery and miracle happen? At the moment of our conception, our parents, with the grace of God, form a unique human person composed of a body and a soul. Then, through Baptism, a person begins to share in God's divine life, having been cleansed of sin and created anew as a child of God. We read about this in the second account of Creation, in which "the LORD

God formed the man out of the dust of the ground and blew into his nostrils the breath of life, and the man became a living being" (Genesis 2:7). This breath of life from God refers to the **soul**. The soul is the invisible, spiritual reality within us that most reflects the image of God in which we are made.

God created humans as a union of a visible, physical body and an invisible, spiritual soul. At the moment we come into being, our spiritual and immortal soul is created immediately by God. Human beings are a combination of body and soul. Our soul animates our being, giving us the ability to reason, to choose, and to will things. Our senses help us to experience the world around us. We have the spiritual ability to know and to love because we each have a soul.

The whole human person, body and soul, is meant to become a temple of the Holy Spirit. One day we will die, but our souls, the breath of God in us, will live forever. At the end of time, our bodies and souls will be reunited when Christ comes again at the Last Judgment.

Did You Know?

Catholics care for themselves, body and soul.

The Church supports and nourishes our faith.

Blaise Pascal, a French mathematician and Catholic theologian, described our desire for God as an "infinite abyss," or space, that only God can fill.

God always takes the first step to fill that space. Faith is our response to God's invitation to share in his life and the way we respond to his call.

For Christians, faith means believing the truth that God has revealed himself to us through his words and actions and, most especially, through Jesus Christ. Faith is a gift from God that guides how we live every day. It is necessary for our salvation. We freely choose to have faith. It is our free response to God, who reveals himself. God does not force it on us.

Faith is also an action—something we do. It is not, however, something we do on our own. No one can believe alone. Faith is not something we can give to ourselves. Faith comes to us in many ways, beginning with God in our families. Do you remember the first prayers you prayed with your family? Do you remember your first experience of Church—going to Mass or celebrating a holy day with your family? Our families help the seed of faith grow in us.

Activity

What is faith? Create a quiz show that has two groups with a moderator. In each round, the groups will complete the sentence:

Faith is _beginning with God_ .

The game is over when each member of both groups has completed the sentence.

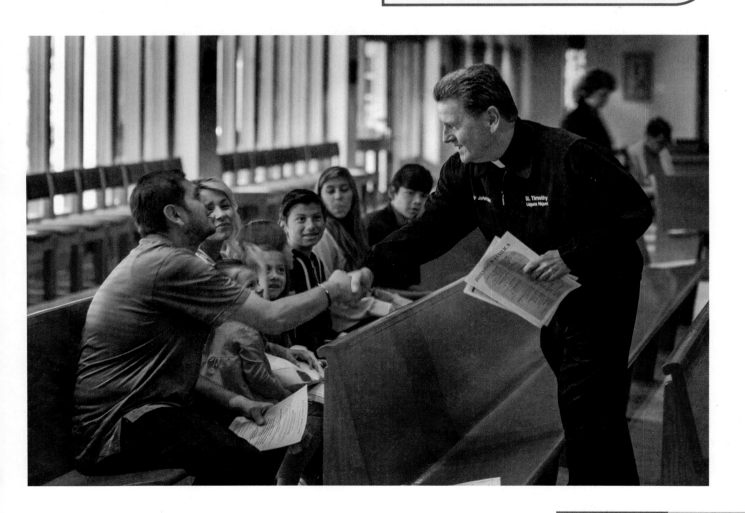

We also experience faith in the Church. The Church teaches us about God, helps us to grow in our knowledge and love of God, and, most especially, nourishes us through the sacraments. In the sacraments, we profess and celebrate everything that we believe and know to be true about God. Through the sacraments, we come to know that God loves us completely and without limit.

- Through faith and the Sacrament of Baptism, we receive new life in Christ.

- In the Sacrament of Confirmation, the outpouring of the Holy Spirit strengthens us to live our faith and be witnesses to God's love in the world.

- In the Sacrament of the Eucharist, we are fed by Christ's Body and Blood.

- In the Sacrament of Penance and Reconciliation, God heals the wounds of sin and division with his forgiveness.

- In the Sacrament of the Anointing of the Sick, God heals us spiritually and gives us hope during times of illness and infirmity.

- In the Sacrament of Matrimony, a man and a woman unite and, through the grace of the sacrament, remain faithful to each other, open to God's gift of children, and committed to raising their children in the faith.

- In the Sacrament of Holy Orders, men are ordained to serve the Church in the Person of Christ. Through the sacrament, they share in the ministerial priesthood of Jesus Christ.

We respond to God by faith when we profess: "I believe."

What Makes Us Catholic?

You might think of the word *nourish* in terms of the food you eat every day, such as bread. As Catholics, we are nourished in a special way during the Communion Rite at Mass. Bread and wine are changed into the Body and Blood of Christ. The bread must be made of wheat and without yeast that would make it rise. The wine has to be made entirely from grapes, with nothing else added. We are not nourished because these items are food and drink. We are nourished by them because they become Christ's own Body and Blood. This is called the Real Presence. We recall Christ's sacrifice and pray for the strength to do his work in the world. When you receive Holy Communion at Sunday Mass, think about what this strength helps you to do.

God created Adam and Eve to live in friendship with him.

When you read the word *paradise*, what images come to mind? Images of the Garden of Eden in Scripture help us to imagine the paradise that God created for Adam and Eve.

Faith Words

original holiness see p. 258
original justice see p. 258
Original Sin see p. 258

> *"The LORD God planted a garden in Eden, in the east, and placed there the man whom he had formed. . . . The LORD God then took the man and settled him in the garden of Eden, to cultivate and care for it."*
>
> Genesis 2:8, 15

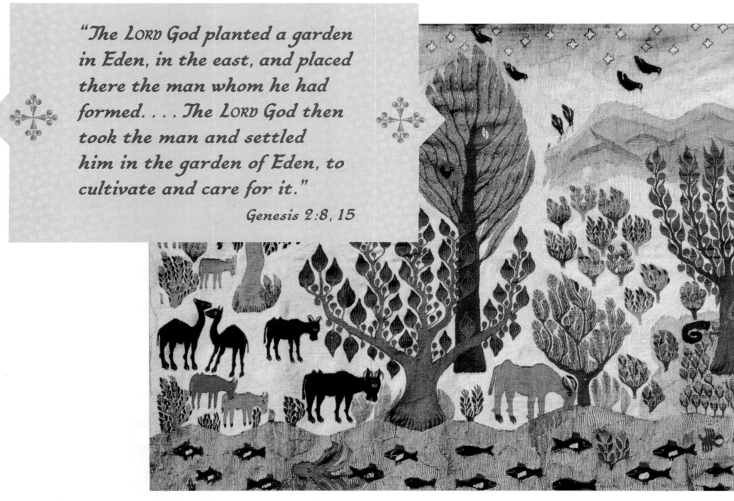

Tree of Knowledge, Adam and Eve in the Garden of Eden **by Karima Ali**

God created Adam and Eve to live in friendship and happiness with him forever. We call this state of being **original holiness**. Original holiness is the original state of human beings in their relationship with God, sharing in the divine life and in full communion with him. This is what God wanted for humans from the beginning.

God created Adam and Eve to live in harmony with themselves, with each other, and with creation. This state of living in harmony is called original justice. **Original justice** is the original

state of Adam and Eve before they disobeyed God. It was a state of complete harmony with themselves, with each other, and with all of creation. This was God's plan for humanity, but it was lost by the sin of our first parents.

Through the Sacrament of Baptism, we are freed from **Original Sin**, the sin of the first man and woman that was passed on to all generations. God invites us to share in his life. Through the sacraments, most especially the Eucharist, we receive the gift of holiness and the grace to live holy lives.

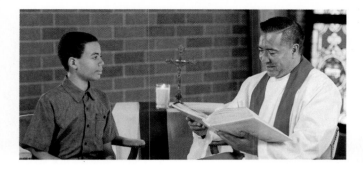

Everyone who dies in God's friendship will have the joy of eternal life with him.

The Church teaches that when we die, Jesus will judge us at the moment of our death on how well we have followed the commandments and his teachings. This is called the **particular judgment**.

"For we must all appear before the judgment seat of Christ, so that each one may receive recompense, according to what he did in the body, whether good or evil" (2 Corinthians 5:10).

Those who have lived holy lives will immediately share in the joy of eternal life, or heaven. Those who still need to grow in holiness will prepare for heaven in Purgatory. And those who have freely chosen to turn away from God and have refused God's mercy and forgiveness will remain separated from God forever. This eternal separation is called hell.

However, God wants all of his children to respond to his grace in their lives. One important way Jesus helps us live holy lives is through the sacraments.

Faith Word

particular judgment see p. 258

One Church, Many Cultures

The Church celebrates November 2 as All Souls' Day. But on November 1 and 2, many Latin American Catholics celebrate Día de los Muertos, or the Day of the Dead. Families often visit the graves of their relatives. They bring crosses, flowers, candles, and other items, and they sometimes play music or read poetry. Afterward, families share a meal to celebrate, remember, and pray for those who have died. Some communities host parades with dancers in costumes.

These special experiences offer graces that configure us to Christ. The Seven Sacraments are seven encounters with God's love and mercy. The sacraments were instituted by Christ to give us the grace we need to be faithful disciples.

Partners in Faith

Saint Peter

Saint Peter was once a fisherman named Simon. One day, he met Jesus and became his follower. Jesus changed Simon's name to *Peter*, which means "the rock." After Jesus' Resurrection, Peter became the representative of Christ on earth, the first of the Apostles and their successors. He is remembered as the first pope. He was martyred in Rome in the first century A.D.

 Learn more about the life of Saint Peter.

Faith Words

soul   original holiness   Original Sin
original justice   particular judgment

 Show What You Know

Complete the sentences.

1. The judgment by God that each person receives at the moment of death is

   the _____ judgment.

2. Original _____ is the original state of human beings'
   relationship with God, sharing in his divine life and in full communion
   with him.

3. The _____ is the invisible spiritual reality within us
   that most reflects the image of God in which we are made.

4. Before Adam and Eve disobeyed God, they were in perfect harmony with him,
   with each other, and with all creation. This is known as

   _____.

5. _____ is the sin of Adam and Eve, passed on to all
   their descendants.

Live Your Faith

• How can you take care of your body?

_____

_____

_____

_____

_____

• How can you take care of your soul?

_____

_____

_____

_____

_____

_____

Mini-Task

Prayer is the principle way we communicate with God.

Talk with a partner about why it is important to take time out of our busy lives for quiet, reflective prayer.

Follow the instructions below to connect with God right at this moment or at any time.

Centering Prayer

Let us recall and become more mindful of how God may be speaking to our hearts.

God has breathed life into us. . . .
Close your eyes and take a deep breath.
Begin by telling God three things you are grateful for in your life right now.
Ask God to help with any needs, hurts, or worries.
Be silent for a few moments.
Conclude by reciting the Lord's Prayer.
Amen.

 Want to do more? Go to your Portfolio to continue this activity.

At Home

Talk with your family members about how you can strengthen one another's faith.

Who is Jesus Christ?

As part of his divine plan of salvation, God willed that his only begotten Son, Jesus, take on human flesh and become like us in all things except sin. Through the power of the Holy Spirit, God prepared Mary to be the mother of his Son. Mary is our model of holiness. The Incarnation is the mystery that God the Son took on a human nature. He is the Savior who came into the world to save us from sin. We share in the new life that Christ won for us.

 Go to the digital portal for a *Lectio* and *Visio Divina* prayer.

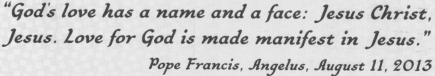

"God's love has a name and a face: Jesus Christ, Jesus. Love for God is made manifest in Jesus."
Pope Francis, Angelus, August 11, 2013

The Holy Spirit prepared Mary for her work as the Mother of God.

Since the beginning, the mission of God the Son and God the Holy Spirit has been at work in the divine plan of salvation. Mary, the Mother of God, is the masterwork of this mission.

By grace, the Holy Spirit prepared Mary to be the mother of God's Son. From the moment of her conception, Mary was free of Original Sin. This is known as the Immaculate Conception. Because she was free of Original Sin and all sin, Mary was able to welcome the "gift of the Almighty" (*CCC*, 722).

Faith Word

Assumption see p. 257

In what way is Mary a model for me?

The Holy Spirit fulfills the plan of God the Father's loving goodness in Mary. Mary accepted God's invitation to participate in his plan of salvation. By the action of the Holy Spirit in Mary, God the Father gave the world Emmanuel, God with us.

We honor the Blessed Virgin Mary as the Mother of God. She was fully united with Jesus her Son from the moment of his conception in her womb. She is a model of faithfulness. The **Assumption** of the Blessed Virgin marks the event in which Mary, at the end of her life, was taken up by God, body and soul, into heaven. In heaven, she shares in the glory of her Son's Resurrection.

One Church, Many Cultures

Latino and Latin American Catholics in the United States have a special connection to Mary as the Blessed Virgin and Mother of God. That connection includes sayings such as *¡Virgen Santísima!* (Holy Virgin) and special Masses to honor Mary. The Cathedral of Our Lady of Divine Providence in Puerto Rico is dedicated to her, and there is a popular devotion to Mary as Our Lady of Guadalupe, whose shrine is in Mexico City. Our Lady of Guadalupe is also the patroness of the Americas.

Activity

Assumption means "to be taken up." *Ascension* means "to rise." Jesus ascended into heaven, but Mary was assumed into heaven. Have a panel discussion to talk about the differences between these two words.

Did You Know?

There are various images of Mary.

The Incarnation is the mystery that Jesus, the only Son of God, became man.

The **Incarnation** is the mystery of the Second Person of the Trinity taking on a human nature. We can never fully understand its meaning: that Jesus had both human knowledge and human will, as we do, *and* a divine knowledge and a divine will.

The Incarnation does *not* mean that Jesus is part God and part man. The Incarnation is the mystery that Jesus became truly man while also remaining truly God.

The events of Jesus' Crucifixion and Resurrection help us understand why this truth is so important. If Jesus was only divine, then his Death on the Cross would not have even been a death as we understand it, because how can God die? The Resurrection would not have been a true rising from the dead.

Jesus, the Son of God, became man to take onto himself our human nature. He offered himself as a sacrifice for our salvation and made us sharers in God's own life.

Faith Word

Incarnation see p. 257

Activity

In the space below, create a mind map of the titles of Jesus. Write a title on the main line and then write words that describe that title. Explain your mind map to a partner.

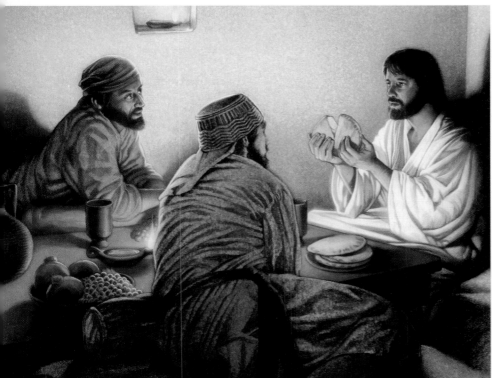

Faith Word

Paschal Mystery see p. 258

Belief in Jesus Christ and his Resurrection changed the disciples' whole way of looking at life. They encountered the Risen Lord after the Resurrection. In those encounters, they knew that death was behind them. Belief in Jesus and his Resurrection changes our whole way of looking at life, too. The life that we now live is not all there is. Jesus shows us the way to eternal life!

Jesus is the Savior who came into the world to save us from sin.

Jesus' victory over death in the Resurrection teaches us that death is not final. Pope Francis described it this way: "Death stands behind us, not before us. Before us is the God of the living . . . the final defeat of sin and death, the beginning of a new time of joy and of endless light. But already on this earth, in prayer, in the Sacraments, in fraternity, we encounter Jesus and his love, and thus we may already taste something of the risen life" (*Angelus*, November 10, 2013).

The Seven Sacraments nourish and strengthen us to live as disciples of Jesus. In the Sacrament of the Eucharist, we share in the **Paschal Mystery**: the life, Death, Resurrection, and Ascension of Jesus Christ. At every moment somewhere in the world, the People of God are celebrating the Sacrament of the Eucharist: the memorial of Christ's work of salvation made present by the liturgical action.

What Makes Us Catholic?

Can you imagine a series of events that makes you want to celebrate all year long? The Paschal Mystery informs our whole Church year. In every season, the Church celebrates and remembers events in the birth, life, suffering, Death, Resurrection, and Ascension of Christ. We celebrate in the Mass and on special occasions, including holy days and feast days. Every time we gather together for these celebrations, we share our belief in Christ and in his return in glory.

Every time we celebrate the Eucharist, we are made sharers in Jesus' Death and Resurrection. This is a great mystery of our faith: Christ is made present to us again. We share in the life of God, the Blessed Trinity.

Christ gave himself in thanksgiving to God the Father when he offered himself on the Cross.

Jesus experienced death so that we might experience divine life with God forever. He poured out the grace of salvation on the Church. We celebrate God's saving action present in the world today.

At the Ascension, the Risen Christ was taken up into heaven.

God revealed himself to us fully in his Son, Jesus Christ. Jesus is our full and complete encounter with God. When we gather as Church to celebrate the sacraments, we encounter Jesus Christ. Through the power of the Holy Spirit, we experience God's saving grace.

Jesus experienced death so that we might experience divine life with God forever. His sacrifice restored us to new life. When we were baptized, we began to share in the Death and Resurrection of Jesus. We were freed from sin and reconciled to God and to each other. In and through Jesus, whose Body and Blood we receive in the Sacrament of the Eucharist, we share in the hope of the Resurrection. The Resurrection of Jesus, which demonstrates his victory over sin and death, holds the promise of our own resurrection, body and soul, and the hope of eternal life.

After his Resurrection, Jesus reminded his disciples of their mission to teach and baptize. He told them to spread the Good News of salvation to the ends of the earth (see Matthew 28:18–20). But forty days after his Resurrection, the time came for Jesus to return to his Father. At his Ascension, Jesus took his place at the Father's right hand. From there, he sent the Holy Spirit upon the Apostles on the feast of Pentecost. He opened the way so that one day we can fully enter into God's life and eternal happiness. The glory of Jesus, "seated at the right hand of the Father" (see the Nicene Creed) is the glory we will see at the end of time, when Christ comes again.

Partners in Faith

Saint Catherine Labouré

Saint Catherine Labouré became a nurse to take care of the sick. One day, the Virgin Mary appeared to her. She asked Saint Catherine to make a medal to honor her. Mary promised that everyone who wore the medal would be blessed. Saint Catherine made the medal, now known as the Miraculous Medal. It shows Mary as the Immaculate Conception. Millions of people wear the medal today to honor Mary and entrust themselves to her care.

 Learn more about the life of Saint Catherine Labouré.

Faith Words

Assumption   **Incarnation**
Paschal Mystery

 ## Show What You Know

Write your own definition for each of the terms below.

1. Paschal Mystery

_____

_____

_____

2. Incarnation

_____

_____

_____

3. Assumption

_____

_____

_____

4. Ascension

_____

_____

_____

Live Your Faith

• What does Christ's Resurrection and Ascension mean to you?

_____

_____

_____

• How would you describe the importance of Jesus' humanity and divinity to a friend who does not know him?

_____

_____

_____

How do I come to know Mary, the Mother of God?

Mini-Task

The Church honors Mary under many titles and descriptions.

Review the truths about Mary found in this lesson. From what you know, write your own title for Mary in the top box below. Add three descriptions of what that title means in the spaces provided and how it can help share a message about Mary with others.

 Want to do more? Go to your Portfolio to continue this activity.

Fearing death is natural, but Christ gives us hope of eternal life. Pray for members of your family who have died.

The Church is the temple of the Holy Spirit and the sacrament of Christ. The Church is made holy by the Holy Spirit. At Baptism we become members of the Church. The Church has a mission from God to proclaim to all people everything that Jesus taught and did. She is guided by the Holy Spirit, motivated by love, and united in celebration of the sacraments, where the saving work of Jesus continues until Jesus comes again in glory.

Go to the digital portal for a prayer of intercession.

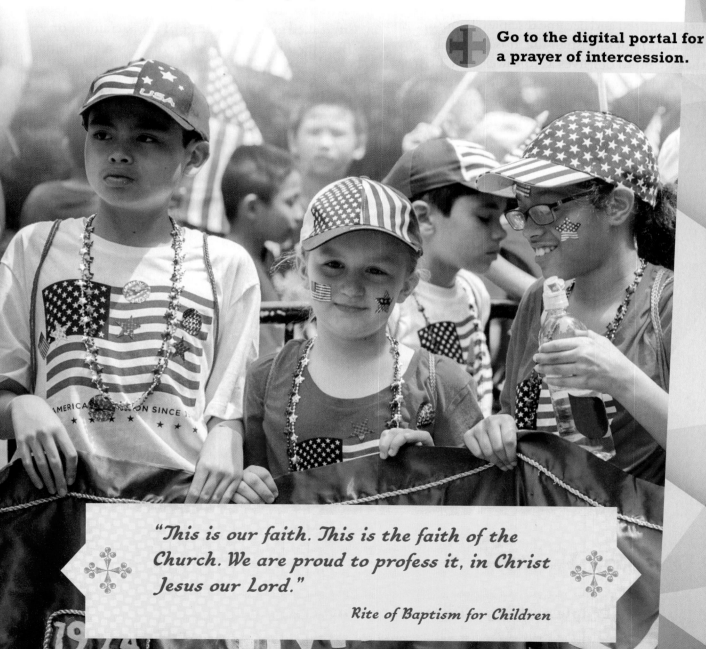

"This is our faith. This is the faith of the Church. We are proud to profess it, in Christ Jesus our Lord."

Rite of Baptism for Children

In Baptism we become members of the Church.

Before he returned to his Father in heaven, Jesus sent his Apostles out to all nations to make disciples, to baptize, and to teach. After Pentecost, the disciples told the crowds that Jesus had died and had risen to new life. They shared their belief that Christ is the Son of God. Peter told the crowds: "Repent and be baptized, every one of you, in the name of Jesus Christ for the forgiveness of your sins; and you will receive the gift of the holy Spirit" (Acts of the Apostles 2:38).

Many people who heard the Good News of Christ were baptized and became disciples. Baptism is the foundation of Christian life. It is upon Baptism that we build our lives as followers of Christ. Baptism is the sacrament in which we are freed from sin, become children of God and sharers in his own life, and are welcomed into the Church.

Faith Words

People of God see p. 258

Church see p. 257

grace see p. 257

In Baptism, we become the **People of God**. We become members of the **Church**, a community led by the Holy Spirit. In this community, no one is more important than anyone else. God sees us all as his children.

When we are baptized, we receive a share in God's life, called **grace**. The grace of the Sacrament of Baptism is necessary for restoring our relationship with God as his sons and daughters.

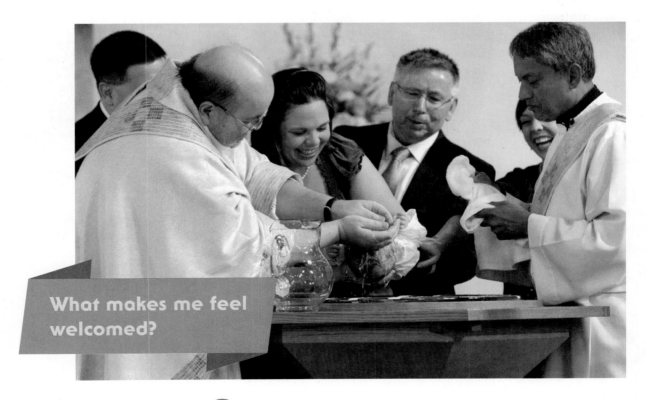

What makes me feel welcomed?

Did You Know?

The People of God gather together in many ways.

The People of God are the temple of the Holy Spirit and the sacrament of Christ.

How would you describe the Catholic Church to a friend who is not Catholic? What would you say? As a start, you can look to the saints for guidance. Saints Peter and Paul used phrases such as the "People of God" and the "temple of the Holy Spirit" to help the first Christians understand the mystery of the Church.

The people of Israel had long understood themselves to be the People of God, God's chosen ones: "I will take you as my own people, and I will be your God" (Exodus 6:7). Peter helped the first Christians understand that they were Christ's chosen ones, the people through whom God would save the world through Christ and the Spirit.

"But you are 'a chosen race, a royal priesthood, a holy nation, a people of his own, so that you may announce the praises' of him who called you out of darkness into his wonderful light" (1 Peter 2:9).

Saint Peter's message was a new one: no one is excluded from the People of God. The Church is open to everyone, no matter who you are or where you come from. People are invited to become members of the Church through Baptism and their profession of faith in Jesus Christ.

Activity

Each of us is a "temple of the holy Spirit" (1 Corinthians 6:19). This means that we need to take good care of our bodies so that they will be a worthy place for the Spirit to dwell. Write four ways you take care of your body.

1. _____

2. _____

3. _____

4. _____

Now choose something you can do to take even better care of your body. Make a plan to do it.

Saint Paul described what it meant to be the People of God. He asked Jesus' followers: "Do you not know that you are the temple of God, and that the Spirit of God dwells in you?" (1 Corinthians 3:16).

Paul was telling the people of Corinth that through Jesus Christ, who has poured out his Spirit, God lives in the Church. His Spirit is the breath of life in the Church and is her source and soul. The Spirit brings unity to the Church and animates, or brings to life, the gifts of the People of God.

The Church is a sacrament of Christ. The Church is a sign of the unity between God and humanity. The Church helps us see God's presence in the world. Through the Church, we can come to know God and share in his plan of salvation.

The Church continues the mission that Jesus gave to his Apostles: to share the Good News of salvation. Through the Church, we share the message of God's truth and love with all people everywhere.

What Makes Us Catholic?

People who have never been baptized join the Church by celebrating the Sacraments of Christian Initiation, usually at the Easter Vigil. Those who have been baptized in another Christian church are not baptized again. This is because Catholics believe in only one Baptism.

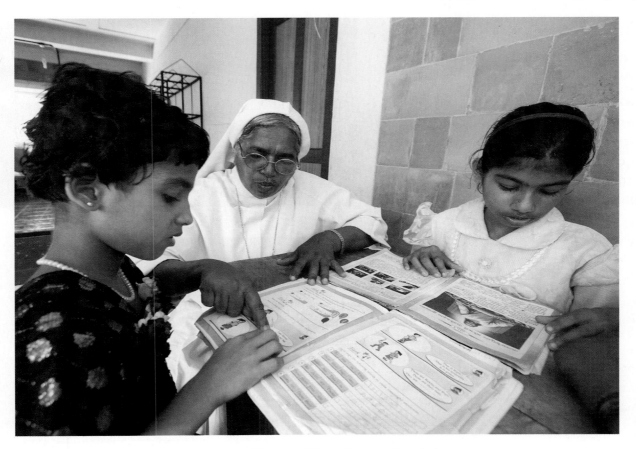

The Syro-Malabar Catholic Missionary Sisters of Mary Immaculate help carry out the Church's mission to spread the Good News of salvation through their work at an orphanage in Kerala, India.

The Church is divinely established, motivated by love, and guided by the Holy Spirit.

Here are some more important things you might tell a friend about the Catholic Church.

- **The Church is divinely established.** The Church has a missionary mandate. This means that Jesus Christ has sent the Church out into the world to preach the Gospel to all people.

- **The Church is motivated by love.** Christ's saving love is at the heart of the Church's mission. The Church proclaims the fullness of faith, completely and without hesitation. The Church proclaims to all people that life with God forever has been made possible through the life, Death, Resurrection, and Ascension of Jesus. The Church is motivated by the love and unity of the Blessed Trinity.

- **The Church is guided by the Holy Spirit.** Guided by the Holy Spirit, the Church lives Christ's mission to bring the Good News to all people. The *Catechism of the Catholic Church* describes how the Church, "urged on by the Spirit of Christ, must walk the road Christ himself walked" (*CCC*, 852).

Activity

Gather in teams to play a trivia game using questions and answers about your parish. Some questions you might ask include:

What saint is my parish named after?
How many Masses does my parish celebrate each week?
How many people belong to my parish?

Research the answer to the questions in advance, and then play the game with another team.

One Church, Many Cultures

Often when there is a natural disaster or another crisis, the Church sends her members to help people all over the world. Catholics bring their skills, talents, and prayers to work in rebuilding homes and businesses, feeding people, and sharing with those in need. For over seventy years, Catholic Relief Services (CRS) has responded to emergencies and helped communities around the world. CRS provides health care, education, and assistance with farming and agriculture, construction, and access to clean water. Wherever the Church goes, she is motivated by God's love. The Church's members show respect and kindness to everyone, regardless of age, race, or beliefs.

Through our Baptism, we continue Jesus' work in the Church today.

Everything Jesus said or did pointed to God's love for us. Jesus treated all people with kindness and mercy. How does the work of Jesus continue in the Church today?

Jesus instituted the sacraments so that his saving work would go on for all time. The sacraments join Catholics all over the world with Jesus and with one another. The Church is a sign of God's love and care, and of the unity of the Blessed Trinity.

Jesus sent his Apostles and their successors out into the world to proclaim the Gospel. He gave them a share in his own mission and the power to act in his name. Bishops—successors of the Apostles—together with the priests and deacons, serve the Church by teaching the faith and celebrating the sacraments.

At Baptism, we are freed from sin. But what about the sins we commit after Baptism? Jesus sent his Apostles to preach repentance and forgiveness of sins in his name. Now bishops and priests have the power to forgive sins through Christ in the Sacrament of Penance and Reconciliation. In this

 Apostles' Creed

sacrament, those who express their sorrow make a firm purpose of amendment, do their penance, confess their sins to a priest, and are forgiven. We also promise to repair the harm caused by our sins. When we receive this sacrament, our relationship with God and the Church is made whole again.

Partners in Faith

Blessed Sára Salkaházi

Blessed Sára Salkaházi was a Hungarian nun who died during World War II. As a young woman, she became a journalist and then joined the Sisters of Social Service. Blessed Sára did charity work, ran a religious bookstore, and established a college for working women. She worked mostly with women and girls. She tried to protect young Jewish women from persecution by the Nazis in Hungary by hiding them in a home for working girls. Blessed Sára's work was discovered, and she was killed by the Nazis.

 Learn more about the life of Blessed Sára Salkaházi.

Faith Words

People of God	Church	grace

 Show What You Know

Unscramble the words to complete the sentences.

ecgar   mlepte   Ppleeo   iritSp

1. _____ is a share in God's life.

2. We are the _____ of God.

3. Saint Paul called the Church the _____ of the Holy Spirit.

4. The Holy _____ guides the Church.

Live Your Faith

• What does it mean to you to be a member of the Church?

_____

_____

_____

_____

_____

_____

_____

_____

_____

• How do you continue Jesus' work in the Church today?

_____

_____

_____

_____

_____

_____

_____

_____

_____

_____

How does my parish reflect the work of the Church?

Mini-Task

Guided by the Holy Spirit, the Church is made up of her members past and present, the People of God, who believe in and follow the teachings of Jesus. That includes you!

Part of being a member of the Church is inviting others to share your faith. On the lines below, write a one-minute commercial for your parish. Your commercial should be about 100 words long. Be sure to include what is special about your parish, how being a member helps you, and why everyone is welcome to join.

_____

_____

_____

_____

_____

_____

_____

_____

_____

_____

_____

 Want to do more? Go to your Portfolio to continue this activity.

Discuss stories of Baptisms in your family. Talk about why it was important to your family to baptize its children.

Unit 2
The Faith Celebrated

The Healing of the Servant

Unit Prayer

Leader: As we learn to celebrate God's love in the world, Saint Ignatius told us that love is shown more in deeds than in words. We tell people how much we love them by the way we act. Through the Mass and sacraments, we learn how to show this love and are able to let the love of Christ live and speak through us.

Let us listen to the stories of missionary disciples among us who show God's love through their lives.

Leader: Let us pray:
O God, your love surrounds us, and we especially know your love through your Son, Jesus. Help us to celebrate your love in the sacraments you have given us.

Reader: O God, help us to celebrate the gift of our Baptism.

All: Help us to be the light of Christ in the world.

Reader: We thank you for your forgiveness.

All: Help us to be the light of Christ in the world.

Reader: Help us to celebrate your love by praying and singing at Mass.

All: Help us to be the light of Christ in the world.

Leader: With Saint Ignatius we pray: "Let our lives be a sign of your love."

All: Let our lives be a sign of your love.

End the Unit Prayer by singing the song for this unit.

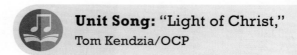

Unit Song: "Light of Christ,"
Tom Kendzia/OCP

Missionary Discipleship

In what way has a part of the celebration of the Mass helped you to show God's love to others? What was it? How did you act? How did you feel?

How does God share his life with us?

So that we would be able to share in God's life and grace, Jesus Christ gave the Church the sacraments. Jesus is with us when we celebrate the liturgy, and the Holy Spirit prepares us to receive Christ in the sacraments. We receive special graces from the Seven Sacraments. Sacramentals help us respond to God's grace that we receive in the sacraments. They are sacred signs that help us on the journey to holiness.

 Go to the digital portal for a litany prayer.

> *"The grace of the Lord Jesus Christ and the love of God and the fellowship of the holy Spirit be with all of you."*
>
> *2 Corinthians 13:13*

Faith Word

liturgy see p. 258

What is one special memory I have from a Mass I have attended?

Jesus is with us when we celebrate the liturgy.

You may wonder: "Why do we have to go to Mass?" A better question might be: "Why would we *not* want to go to Mass?" Jesus is there in the most special way. He is waiting to fill us to the brim with his love.

Every time the Church gathers to celebrate the liturgy, Jesus is present. The **liturgy** is the work of Christ and his Church. Jesus is at work in every liturgy, drawing us closer to God the Father, through the power of the Holy Spirit. Jesus is with us, making present his Paschal Mystery. Through the power of the Holy Spirit, we participate in this mystery of our salvation.

Christ acts through the liturgy, particularly the sacraments, to communicate God's grace to us. He is always there with us, pouring out God's life upon us.

Did You Know?

 Mass is celebrated in various languages.

The Holy Spirit prepares us to receive Christ in the sacraments.

Faith Word

sacraments see p. 258

In the liturgy, the People of God encounter the Father, the Son, and the Holy Spirit. The Holy Spirit calls us together and prepares us to meet Christ. In the liturgy of the Church, the Holy Spirit is our teacher. The *Catechism of the Catholic Church* calls the Holy Spirit the "artisan of 'God's masterpieces,'" the sacraments (*CCC*, 1091).

In the **sacraments**, the Holy Spirit recalls the mystery of Christ. Together with the Church, the Spirit manifests, or makes known, Christ and his work of salvation. This is why the Church teaches that "the Holy Spirit is the Church's living memory" (*CCC*, 1099).

The Holy Spirit prepares our hearts and minds to encounter Jesus when we celebrate the sacraments. This preparation is the joint work of the Holy Spirit and all those gathered, especially the ministers. The Holy Spirit works within us to awaken our faith, turn our hearts to God, and give us the grace to know what God wants for us.

Activity

The following are some of the roles of the Holy Spirit in the Church. Write what they mean to you.

Teacher _____

Advocate _____

Life-giver _____

What role do you want the Holy Spirit to have in your life right now? Share your answer with a partner.

How is the Holy Spirit at work in the sacraments? When we celebrate the sacraments, we are not simply recalling the events that saved us. Instead, these events are made present through the outpouring of the Holy Spirit.

For example, in the Liturgy of the Word during the Mass, the Holy Spirit is present in the Word of God. The Holy Spirit opens our hearts and helps us to understand the meaning of what we hear so that we may live out that meaning in our daily lives. The Holy Spirit awakens our memory of everything that Christ has done for us.

During the Liturgy of the Eucharist, the priest asks God the Father to send the Holy Spirit so that the offerings of bread and wine may become the Body and Blood of Christ. This calling or "invocation of" the Holy Spirit is at the heart of each sacramental celebration, especially the Eucharist.

The Holy Spirit is present in every sacrament, working to bring us into communion with Christ and to form his Body, the Church.

What Makes Us Catholic?

The Catholic Church celebrates the Seven Sacraments: Baptism, Confirmation, Eucharist, Penance and Reconciliation, Anointing of the Sick, Holy Orders, and Matrimony. Baptism, Confirmation, and the Eucharist are Sacraments of Christian Initiation. They are the foundation of our life in Jesus. Through Penance and Anointing of the Sick, the Church continues Christ's work of healing and forgiving sins. Holy Orders and Matrimony are Sacraments at the Service of Communion. Those who celebrate them help the Church's mission by their service to others.

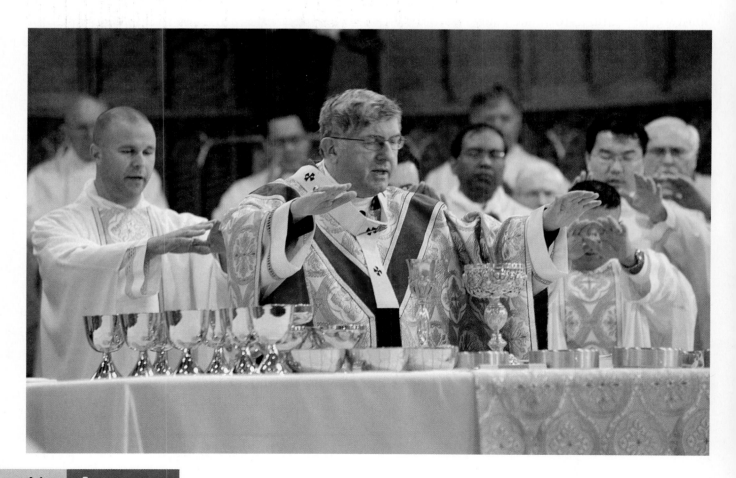

The Church shares signs of God's grace primarily through the sacraments.

The Seven Sacraments are celebrations that are special signs of God's love, presence, and saving power. Jesus instituted the sacraments. He gave them to the Church so that his saving work would continue for all time.

The sacraments are different from all other signs. Sacraments truly bring about what they represent. For example, we not only celebrate being children of God during Baptism, we also actually become children of God. This is why we say that a sacrament is an effective sign of grace instituted by Christ and entrusted to the Church, by which divine life is shared with us.

Christ is at work in the sacraments. Each sacrament offers unique sacramental graces that allow us to participate in God's divine life. This grace helps us to trust and believe in God. It strengthens us to live as Jesus did. We receive special graces from each of the sacraments when we celebrate them properly.

Activity

The Seven Sacraments are celebrations of God's love and presence. As a group, talk about what comes to mind when each of the sacraments is named.

Baptism • Confirmation • Eucharist

Penance and Reconciliation • Anointing of the Sick

Holy Orders • Matrimony

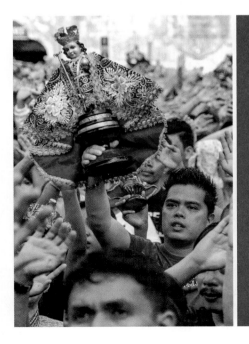

One Church, Many Cultures

Many Filipino-American Catholics participate in a devotion to Santo Niño de Cebu, the Holy Child Jesus. In Cebu, Philippines, dating back to 1565, a statue of Jesus as a child is the site of the largest gathering for this devotion. There is a copy of this statue in St. Augustine Catholic Church in Philadelphia. In the United States and other countries, a statue representing the Santo Niño is dressed in bright clothing for the Feast of Santo Niño, or Sinulog. The nine-day devotion begins with a parade and ends with a Mass. It includes a closing procession with members of the assembly holding images of the Santo Niño.

Sacramentals are sacred signs instituted by the Church.

Faith Word

sacramentals see p. 258

What might you find in a Catholic home on the walls or in other places? A crucifix, a Bible, a statue of Mary, the Blessed Mother, a Guardian Angel plaque, an icon of a saint? And why would you find these particular items in a Catholic home? These objects are **sacramentals**.

Sacramentals are blessings, actions, and objects that help us respond to God's grace. Blessings are the most important sacramentals. Not only is the blessing itself a sacramental, but what is blessed can also become a sacramental. Blessings praise God for his works and gifts.

Sacramentals are used in the liturgy and in personal prayer. Here are some examples of sacramentals:

• blessings of people, places, foods, and objects
• objects such as rosaries, medals, crucifixes, blessed ashes, and blessed palms
• actions such as making the Sign of the Cross and sprinkling blessed water

Sacramentals seek to sanctify special moments of our lives or particular ministries in the Church. Many sacramentals remind us of the sacraments and of what God does for us through the sacraments. Sacramentals also make us more aware of God's presence in our lives and keep us focused on God. In particular, they prepare us to receive God's grace and cooperate with it. Sacramentals can help make every event in our lives holy. Blessing the food we eat, making the Sign of the Cross as we enter or leave a church, and seeing a crucifix in our home are all reminders that God is with us.

Partners in Faith

Saint Elizabeth Ann Seton

Saint Elizabeth Ann Seton is the first saint born in the United States. She was raised as a Protestant in New York. After her husband died, she joined the Catholic Church. She founded the first Catholic girls school in the United States. Soon other women joined her, and she started the Sisters of Charity to work with poor children.

 Learn more about the life of Saint Elizabeth Ann Seton.

Faith Words

| liturgy | sacraments | sacramentals |

 Show What You Know

Complete the sentences.

1. Blessings, actions, and objects that help us respond to God's grace in

the sacraments are called _____ .

2. _____ are effective signs instituted by Christ
and entrusted to the Church, by which divine life is shared with us.

3. The _____ prepares our hearts and minds to
encounter Jesus in the sacraments.

4. The _____ is the work and prayer of the
whole Church.

Live Your Faith

• What does the gift of grace that you receive in the sacraments do for you?

_____

_____

_____

_____

_____

_____

_____

_____

• How are you a part of the liturgy?

_____

_____

_____

_____

_____

_____

_____

_____

Where do I meet Jesus?

Mini-Task

Jesus is really and truly present in the celebration of the liturgy. He is present in the ministers, in the Word, and in the People of God gathered to celebrate. Christ is present in a unique and real way in the Eucharist.

How are you changed by encountering the Real Presence of Jesus at Mass?

How do you share his love on an average day?

Plan a one-minute video testimonial about the way or ways you feel changed by meeting Jesus.

On the lines below, write a brief script for your video.

_____

_____

_____

_____

_____

_____

_____

_____

_____

_____

 Want to do more? Go to your Portfolio to continue this activity.

 At Home

Through the Holy Spirit's action, we are drawn close to Jesus and receive grace. We are drawn close to one another, too. The next time your family goes to Mass, take a minute to look around. Remember that every person there is your brother or sister in Christ.

How do we praise and thank God?

The Church praises and thanks God all year long with sacramental celebrations. Those celebrations include the Mass, where we learn about God's love for his people in the Liturgy of the Word. Throughout the year, we participate in liturgical celebrations and in the Church's blessings and devotions, when we worship God and honor holy people.

Go to the digital portal for a prayer of petition.

"The celebration of Mass, as the action of Christ and of the People of God . . . is the center of the whole of Christian life for the Church . . . moreover, during the course of the year, the mysteries of redemption are celebrated so as to be in some way made present."

Roman Missal, 1.16

We learn about God's love for his people in the Liturgy of the Word.

Liturgy is the gathering of the Church, the Body of Christ, to worship God. It is the official, public prayer of the Church. We gather to bless and adore God the Father, who is the source of all the blessings of creation. We worship and adore God, who offers us salvation, blesses us with his Son, and invites us to be his children.

The most important liturgy of the Church is the Mass, in which we gather to celebrate the Eucharist. Through the power of the Holy Spirit, we join with Jesus in giving thanks and praise to God the Father.

An essential part of the Mass is the **Liturgy of the Word**. This is the part of the Mass in which we listen and respond to God's Word.

Faith Word

Liturgy of the Word
see p. 258

On Sundays, we listen and respond to Scripture readings from the Old Testament and the New Testament. We pray the Responsorial Psalm from the Book of Psalms. We hear about God's great love for his people in the First Reading, usually taken from the Old Testament. We hear about the life and teaching of Christ in the Second Reading, from the New Testament. The proclamation of the Gospel is the high point of the Liturgy of the Word, because it ordinarily includes the words of Jesus himself. After the Gospel, the priest or deacon helps us to understand God's Word and apply it to our lives. We profess our faith and pray for all people in need.

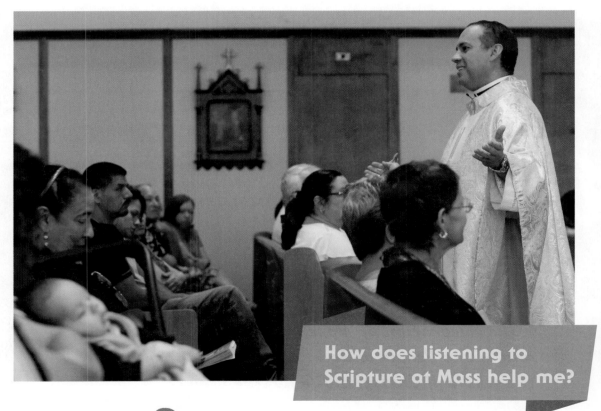

How does listening to Scripture at Mass help me?

Did You Know?

 The Liturgy of the Word has many parts.

Faith Word

liturgical year see p. 258

Our Lady of Kamalen is the patron saint of Guam.

We worship God and honor holy people throughout the liturgical year.

The Church has special days and times of the year that are important. We remember these times in the celebration of the liturgy. In the liturgy throughout the year, we remember and rejoice in the saving actions of Jesus Christ. The calendar that guides the liturgies and celebrations of the Church year is called the **liturgical year**.

During the liturgical year, we recall and celebrate the whole mystery of Jesus Christ. We celebrate the birth of the Son of God and his younger years, public ministry, suffering, Death, Resurrection, and Ascension into heaven. We celebrate the coming of the Holy Spirit upon the Apostles at Pentecost. And during the year we venerate, or show devotion to, Mary, the Mother of God, and to all the saints.

The Church honors the Blessed Virgin Mary, Mother of God, with a special love. Because she is so closely connected to the saving work of Jesus, the Church admires and raises her up as a model of discipleship. Everything Mary says and does points us to her Son: "Do whatever he tells you" (John 2:5). This is why, throughout the liturgical year, we celebrate the Marian holy days and feast days.

The Church also honors saints during the liturgical year. The saints are holy men and women who have suffered and been glorified in Christ. Their lives of holiness show us what it means to enter into the Paschal Mystery. The Church holds up the saints as models of faithfulness. They teach us what it means to live the Gospel. Their lives draw us closer to God the Father, through Christ.

Activity

Use the definitions to identify feasts and seasons of the liturgical year. Work with a partner and discuss why certain colors are associated with the feasts and seasons.

Celebration of the Resurrection

Coming of the Holy Spirit

Third Sunday of Advent

Time for growing and learning

Time of penance

Time of waiting before Christmas

The Church's worship and celebrations are connected by Apostolic Tradition.

If you visit a parish for Mass on the other side of the world, you will likely experience liturgical traditions different from your own. This is because Catholic churches in different areas of the world celebrate the mystery of Christ in ways that are reflective of their cultures. They celebrate the same truth—the same Paschal Mystery—just a bit differently! These liturgical differences actually enrich the Church. The *Catechism of the Catholic Church* tells us: "The mystery of Christ is so unfathomably rich that it cannot be exhausted by its expression in any single liturgical tradition" (*CCC*, 1201).

At the same time, many things about the celebration of Mass on the other side of the world will be familiar to you. This is because the Church celebrates the same Paschal Mystery: the Passion, Death, Resurrection, and Ascension of Jesus. From the first Pentecost to today, we celebrate the one faith received from the Apostles and passed down through Apostolic Tradition.

One Church, Many Cultures

The Church in Tanzania shares similar cultural connections to other Catholic churches in Africa. The Mass is celebrated over several hours. It often features singing and dancing in front of the altar between the solemn ritual celebrations. There are extended prayer petitions. Feast day liturgical celebrations can include long processions that pause for more singing and dancing, and prayer before the Eucharist. Masses during the Christmas season and throughout the New Year feature longer homilies from the priest and begin several hours before midnight.

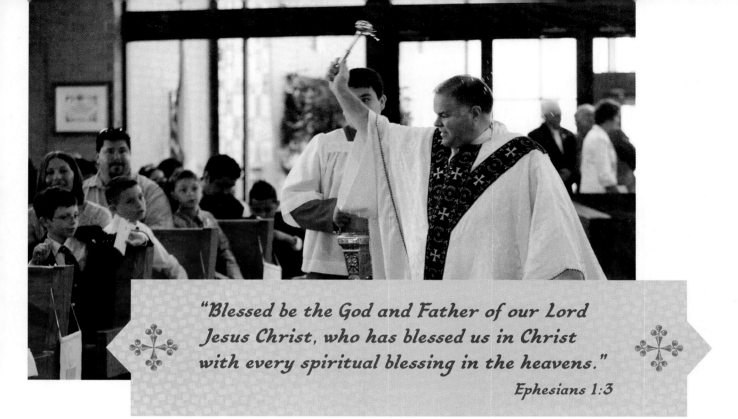

> *"Blessed be the God and Father of our Lord Jesus Christ, who has blessed us in Christ with every spiritual blessing in the heavens."*
>
> Ephesians 1:3

Blessings and devotions honor God and our models of holiness.

Of all the many different kinds of sacramentals—blessings, actions, and objects that help us respond to God's grace in the sacraments—blessings "come first" (*CCC*, 1671). In other words, blessings are the most important sacramental. Many blessings invoke the Blessed Trinity with a sign of the cross and often involve a sprinkling of holy water.

A blessing is a prayer that praises God and prays for his gifts. Through Jesus Christ, Christians are blessed by God the Father.

Activity

Blessings are the most important sacramentals. Write a short blessing for a friend and another for one of the following:

- your mother
- your father
- your teacher
- your friend

What Makes Us Catholic?

At some Masses, the priest blesses us during a Sprinkling Rite. He uses a sprinkling of holy water from an *aspergillum*, a liturgical item that looks like a silver ball on a stick or a brush. The priest casts the holy water as he walks through the church, sprinkling himself, any other ministers, and the assembly. This rite is called the Asperges. In some cultures, the water may contain salt that has also been blessed. This sprinkling reminds us of our Baptism. The Sprinkling Rite is often part of the Mass during the season of Easter.

Every person is called to be a blessing, and every person is called to bless. We can both bless others and receive blessings from others. Blessings for students at the start of a new school year, for the teenager who just received his or her driver's license, or for the young adult moving away from home— all these are blessings for new beginnings. There are blessings for just about every situation in life.

Devotions and forms of popular piety draw us closer to God. Many devotions honor holy men and women whose lives are models of discipleship. Devotions such as the Stations of the Cross, the Rosary, pilgrimages, processions, and lighting candles at church nourish our faith. They also prepare our hearts and minds for the celebration of the sacraments.

Partners in Faith

Blessed Victoire Rasoamanarivo

Victoire Rasoamanarivo was a member of the royal family of Madagascar. Her parents sent her to Catholic school, where she learned about Jesus. She became a Catholic when she was 15 years old, even though her parents disapproved. She married a man who was cruel to her, but she prayed for his conversion. After his death, she cared for the poor and sick.

 Learn more about the life of Blessed Victoire Rasoamanarivo.

Faith Words

Liturgy of the Word   **liturgical year**

 ## Show What You Know

In your own words, write definitions for the terms.

liturgical year

_____

_____

_____

_____

Liturgy of the Word

_____

_____

_____

_____

_____

Which of the following is a devotion?

  a. Stations of the Cross
  b. liturgy
  c. Paschal Mystery

Live Your Faith

• Why are many aspects of the Church's celebrations around the
world the same?

_____

_____

_____

_____

• Who in your life needs to receive a blessing? Why?

_____

_____

_____

_____

_____

How does faith connect me with others?

Mini-Task

Imagine that you are starting a blog for Catholic young people all over the world. Part of your blog will be a forum in which visitors are invited to share their faith stories and experiences in the Church.

Organize the structure of your forum. Develop five questions that will lead the forum. Write them below. Make them interesting and pertinent to young people's lives to spark conversation and response. Share your forum questions with the group.

 Want to do more? Go to your Portfolio to continue this activity.

At Home

With your family, find the readings for next Sunday's Mass in a Bible or online. Try to find time to read together and pray about those Scriptures before Mass.

How do we become members of the Church?

The Sacraments of Initiation—Baptism, Confirmation, and Eucharist—are the foundation of the Christian life. These sacraments begin, strengthen, and nourish our life of faith. Through Baptism, we are configured in Christ, freed from Original Sin, and forgiven for any personal sin. We are born into new life in Christ and become members of the Church. The Sacrament of Confirmation seals us with the Gift of the Holy Spirit. In the Eucharist, the memorial of Christ's sacrifice, we are nourished by the Real Presence of Christ.

Go to the digital portal for a prayer of petition.

"*Lord God,*
. . . Bless all your adopted children
and add these chosen ones
to the harvest of your new covenant. . . .
may they rejoice in eternal life,
won, not by the power of nature,
but through the mystery of your grace."
Rite of Christian Initiation of Adults

The Sacraments of Christian Initiation begin, strengthen, and nourish our life in the Church.

Christian initiation is the process of becoming a member of the Church. The Sacraments of Baptism, Confirmation, and Eucharist initiate us into the Church. They are the **Sacraments of Christian Initiation**.

The Sacrament of Baptism is the first sacrament we receive. In Baptism we are united to Christ and become part of the Body of Christ and the People of God. The celebration of this first Sacrament of Christian Initiation is very important. In fact, we are unable to receive any other sacrament until we first have been baptized. Baptism is our welcome into new life in Christ and into the Church.

In the Sacrament of Confirmation, we are sealed with the Gift of the Holy Spirit. Confirmation continues what Baptism has begun. We are strengthened to live as Christ's followers.

The Sacrament of the Eucharist is the Sacrament of the Body and Blood of Christ. The Eucharist is connected to our Baptism, too. Each time we receive Holy Communion, our bonds as the Body of Christ are made stronger. Our community of faith is nourished by God's life.

Faith Word

Sacraments of Christian Initiation see p. 258

What did I experience when attending a Baptism or Confirmation?

What Makes Us Catholic?

After we celebrate the Liturgy of the Eucharist at Mass, any hosts that remain or are reserved for those who will receive it outside of Mass are placed inside a container or cabinet called the tabernacle. The Real Presence of Christ remains true and real in the consecrated hosts. We can spend time with the Real Presence in this way during Eucharistic adoration. This is a devotion in which the priest places a consecrated host in a special holder called a monstrance, and we pray in front of it. In adoration, we focus our thoughts on Christ and his sacrifice for us.

Did You Know?

 In the Rite of Election, it is God who chooses us.

Baptism gives us a special grace to share in the life and work of Jesus.

The **Sacrament of Baptism** is the foundation of Christian life. It is the very first sacrament that we celebrate. Baptism leads us to the other two Sacraments of Christian Initiation: Confirmation and Eucharist. It is upon Baptism that we build our lives as followers of Christ. We receive the Gift of the Holy Spirit and share in God's own life, which is God's grace. The grace of Baptism helps us to believe in God the Father and to love him. It strengthens us to live as Jesus' disciples in the world.

Jesus said: "No one can enter the kingdom of God without being born of water and Spirit" (John 3:5). The *Catechism of the Catholic Church* tells us that Baptism is "necessary for salvation, as is the Church herself, which we enter by Baptism" (*CCC*, 1277).

Through the Sacrament of Baptism:

• We are freed from Original Sin and any personal sins are forgiven.

• We become adopted children of God.

• We are joined to Christ and rise to new life in him.

• We become members of the Church, the Body of Christ.

• We are united with all others who have been baptized.

• We are justified, or brought into right relationship with God.

• We are sharers in God's own life.

• We become temples of the Holy Spirit.

There are times when a person who is near death or in danger of dying may want to be baptized. If a priest or deacon is not available, any person, even someone not baptized, can baptize. He or she must intend to do what the Church does. The person must follow the essential rite of the sacrament, which is the pouring of water three times on the person's head, with the words "I baptize you in the name of the Father, and of the Son, and of the Holy Spirit" (*Rite of Baptism*, 60).

Faith Word

Baptism see p. 257

Activity

In an emergency, if a person wants to be baptized but a priest or deacon isn't available, you can baptize the person.

Put the following steps in the correct order.

3	Pour water on the person's head three times.
1	Ask if the person wants to be baptized.
2	Say the words from the Rite of Baptism.

The Sacrament of Confirmation seals us with the Gift of the Holy Spirit.

God the Holy Spirit is always with the Church. We first receive the Gift of the Holy Spirit at our Baptism. In the **Sacrament of Confirmation**, we are sealed with the Gift of the Holy Spirit. We become more like Christ and are strengthened to be his witnesses.

 Come, Holy Spirit

On Pentecost, the Holy Spirit came upon the Apostles (see Acts of the Apostles 2:1–4). The Holy Spirit strengthened and guided them to give witness to Christ. They baptized many believers. Those people received the strengthening power of the Holy Spirit when the Apostles placed their hands on them. The **laying on of hands** was a sign of God's blessing. By this action, authority and grace were given in God's name.

The laying on of hands by the Apostles was the beginning of the Sacrament of Confirmation. As the Church's understanding of the sacrament developed, an anointing was joined to the laying on

of hands. The word *anoint* means "to apply oil to someone as a sign that God has chosen that person for a special mission." Like the laying on of hands, anointing is an ancient practice. Anointing was an important part of Jewish life during Jesus' time.

The anointing that happened with the laying on of hands was a sign of the Holy Spirit's outpouring on the person. In time, the anointing became the essential sign of the Gift of the Holy Spirit. **Sacred Chrism**, oil blessed by a bishop, was used in this anointing. Today, in the Sacrament of Confirmation, the anointing with Sacred Chrism is done as the bishop anoints the forehead of the person being confirmed.

Faith Words

Confirmation see p. 257

laying on of hands see p. 257

anoint see p. 257

Sacred Chrism see p. 258

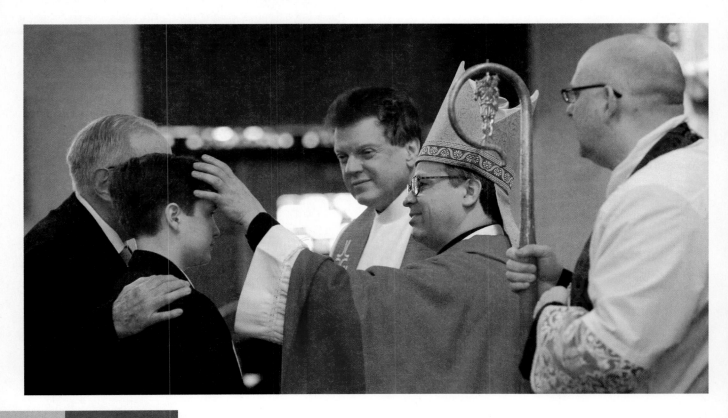

The Sacrament of Confirmation completes Baptism. Like Baptism, it configures us more closely to Christ. And like Baptism, we receive Confirmation only once. However, the time varies in a person's life when it can be received.

In the Roman Catholic Church, people who were baptized as infants generally receive Confirmation between the ages of 10 and 15. The Eastern Catholic Churches celebrate Confirmation at the time of Baptism (infancy), followed by the Eucharist. This tradition highlights the unity of the three Sacraments of Initiation. Adults and older children who are preparing for Baptism receive the Sacrament of Confirmation as a part of the Rite of Christian Initiation.

The Sacrament of Confirmation deepens the grace we first received at Baptism. In Confirmation:

- We are sealed with the Gift of the Holy Spirit.
- We become more like Jesus and are strengthened to be active witnesses.
- Our friendship with God the Father is deepened.
- Our relationship with the Church is strengthened.
- We are sent forth to live our faith in the world.

Activity

Use the Faith Words on page 82 in sentences. Share what each means in order to tell others why Holy Communion is one of the greatest gifts God has given us.

- Consecration
- transubstantiation
- Real Presence

One Church, Many Cultures

In Baptism, the parents of the baptized infant name godparents for their children. Godparents ensure that the child will be protected and raised to know God. Godparents have a special significance in the Latino Church, remaining involved in the lives of the godchildren well past the teenage years. *Padrinos* typically buy a christening gown and candle for the infant. They also offer their godchildren special gifts over the years, including items that promote and encourage their faith. *Padrinos* also serve as *compadres*, or "co-parents," offering advice and love.

In the Eucharist, we are nourished by the Real Presence of Christ.

At the Last Supper, Jesus gave us the gift of himself in the Eucharist. Through the Eucharist, Jesus remains with us forever. The Eucharist is the Sacrament of the Body and Blood of Christ. Jesus is truly present under the appearances of bread and wine. It is the only Sacrament of Christian Initiation that we receive more than once. We honor Jesus by remembering what he did for us, sharing in the Last Supper, and remembering his Passion, Death, Resurrection, and Ascension.

Jesus told his Apostles to "do this in memory of me" (Luke 22:19). When we gather and break bread, we remember the new life we have because of Jesus' Death and Resurrection. In this way, the Eucharist is a memorial. But it is much more than just remembering past events. In the Eucharist, Christ is really present, and so is his sacrifice on Calvary more than two thousand years ago.

By the power of the Holy Spirit, the Paschal Mystery—Christ's Passion, Death, Resurrection, and Ascension—is made present to us. We join Jesus in offering ourselves to God the Father. We offer our joys, worries, and willingness to live as Jesus' disciples.

Jesus acts through the priest to offer the sacrifice of the Eucharist. A sacrifice is a gift offered to God by a priest in the name of all the people. In the case of the Eucharist, the priest is ordained to act in the person of Christ, the High Priest. It is Christ who

Faith Words

Consecration see p. 257

transubstantiation see p. 259

Real Presence see p. 258

offers the sacrifice. The priest celebrates the Eucharist for and with the People of God. At the **Consecration**, by the power of the Holy Spirit and through the words and actions of the priest, the bread and wine really become the Body and Blood of Christ. Though they still appear to the senses as bread and wine, their substance has changed. This change is called **transubstantiation**. Jesus is fully present in the Eucharist, in Body, Blood, soul, and divinity. This is known as the **Real Presence**. When we receive Holy Communion, we are nourished by the Body and Blood of Christ. Jesus lives in us and we live in him.

In the Sacrament of the Eucharist:

• We are nourished by the Word of God and receive Jesus Christ in Holy Communion.

• We are joined more closely to Christ and one another.

• The grace received in Baptism grows in us.

• We are strengthened to love and serve others.

Partners in Faith

Saint Teresa of the Andes

Saint Teresa of the Andes is the first saint from Chile. As a child, she had a temper and did not get along with her brothers and sisters. After reading about Saint Thérèse of Lisieux, she wanted to follow her example. She entered the convent but died when she was only 19 years old.

 Learn more about the life of Saint Teresa of the Andes.

Faith Words

Sacraments of Christian Initiation
Baptism   Confirmation
laying on of hands   anoint
Sacred Chrism   Consecration
transubstantiation   Real Presence

 ## Show What You Know

Match the terms to the correct definitions.

1. Confirmation

2. transubstantiation

3. Sacraments of
   Christian Initiation

4. Sacred Chrism

5. Consecration

6. Real Presence

the change of bread and wine into the Body and
Blood of Christ

the point during the Eucharistic Prayer when the
bread and wine become the Body and Blood of Christ

oil blessed by the bishop

the sacrament in which we receive the Gift of the
Holy Spirit in a special way

Christ's true and real presence in the Eucharist in
the form of bread and wine

these welcome us into the Church

Live Your Faith

• What do the laying on of hands and anointing signify in the Sacrament of Confirmation?

_____

_____

_____

_____

_____

_____

_____

• What does the Eucharist give you the strength to do?

_____

_____

_____

Mini-Task

Baptism is the foundation of our life of faith. It is the first of the Sacraments of Initiation, in which we are welcomed into the Church.

You probably do not remember your Baptism if you were a baby, but you have experienced many graces as a child of God since that time.

On the lines below, design a spiritual timeline with moments when you have experienced the grace of God in your life.

_____

_____

_____

_____

_____

_____

_____

_____

_____

_____

_____

_____

 Want to do more? Go to your Portfolio to continue this activity.

 At Home

Talk with your family members about what's going on in your lives right now. Be respectful of one another. Include the good and the bad. Offer a prayer of love and comfort for everyone in your family.

How do we celebrate God's forgiveness and healing?

In the Gospels, Jesus showed that God has power over sickness and sin. The Church celebrates God's healing and forgiveness in the Sacrament of Penance and Reconciliation and the Sacrament of Anointing of the Sick—the Sacraments of Healing. In the Sacrament of Penance and Reconciliation, Jesus forgives sin through the ministry of priests and bishops. The sacrament heals us of the damage to our relationship with God caused by sin. It strengthens us to live as God wants us to live. In the Sacrament of the Anointing of the Sick, God's healing grace is given to those who are sick, suffering, or near death.

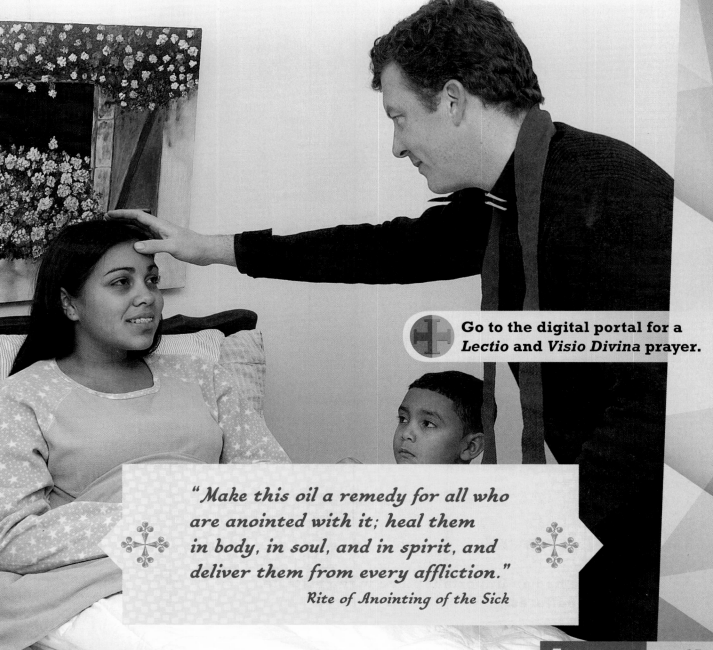

Go to the digital portal for a *Lectio* and *Visio Divina* prayer.

"Make this oil a remedy for all who are anointed with it; heal them in body, in soul, and in spirit, and deliver them from every affliction."
Rite of Anointing of the Sick

We celebrate and receive God's healing in a special way.

Healing was an important part of Jesus' ministry from the very beginning. Many people grew to believe in Jesus because of his healing. Jesus' healing was a sign of God's presence and action in the lives of people.

Jesus cared about the needs of all people. However, he had a special concern for those who were sick and suffering. He did not ignore people who had diseases or disabilities. He listened to them and treated them with respect.

Jesus also wanted to heal people from sin. Often when he cured the sick, he also forgave their sins. Jesus forgave the sins of people because he knew that sin kept them from loving God and living life to the fullest.

The healing and forgiving actions of Jesus showed others that he was the Son of God. They showed that the Kingdom of God was close at hand. Jesus' actions showed that God has power over sickness and sin. Jesus' healing of the sick and forgiveness of sin are signs of his power to save us and bring us God's life.

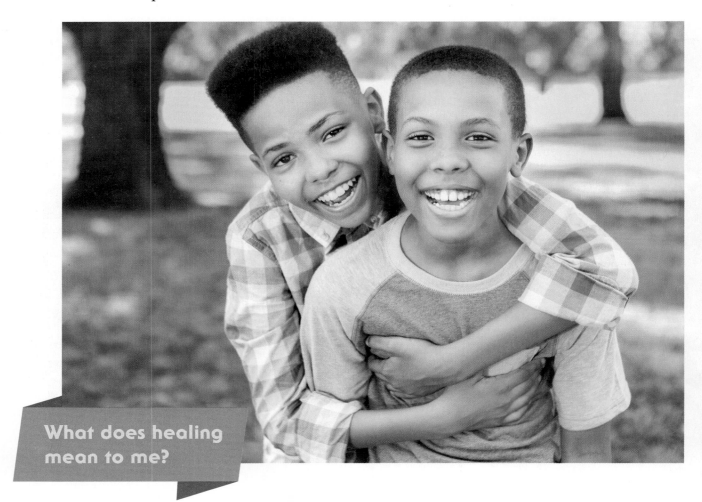

What does healing mean to me?

Did You Know?

Oils have had an important place in the histories of many cultures.

Faith Words

Penance and Reconciliation
see p. 258

Sacraments of Healing
see p. 258

Jesus forgives our sins and heals us through the Sacrament of Penance and Reconciliation.

Jesus gave the Church the **Sacraments of Healing**: Penance and Anointing of the Sick. The **Sacrament of Penance and Reconciliation** continues Jesus' ministry of healing and forgiveness. When we sin, we turn away from God, the source of life. An attachment to sin keeps us from the joy and fullness of life God wants for us. We were created for God, and God is love. Sin keeps us from experiencing and sharing the love of God more fully. Venial sin hurts our relationship with God but does not break it. Mortal sin separates us from God. To commit a mortal sin, the sin must be (1) serious in nature, (2) the person must know he or she is committing a sin, and (3) the person must freely choose to commit the sin.

In the Sacrament of Penance, which we also call Confession, we are healed of both venial sin and mortal sin. We are required to confess mortal sin in Confession.

The Sacrament of Penance is a sacrament of conversion. It redirects us toward God. Conversion means changing our focus and our spiritual goals and choosing to turn back to God. This conversion leads us to repent, or to be sorry for our sins. This repentance is known as contrition.

What Makes Us Catholic?

The Anointing of the Sick often takes place outside the celebration of the Mass. As a result, the sacrament usually begins with a Liturgy of the Word and is followed by Holy Communion if possible. In this way, those being anointed are further strengthened and nourished by the Word of God and by the Body and Blood of Christ. Holy Communion also joins those who are suffering to their parish community, even when they are unable to attend Mass.

> "When [Jesus] entered Capernaum, a centurion approached him and appealed to him, saying, 'LORD, my servant is lying at home paralyzed, suffering dreadfully.' He said to him, 'I will come and cure him.'"
>
> Matthew 8:5–7

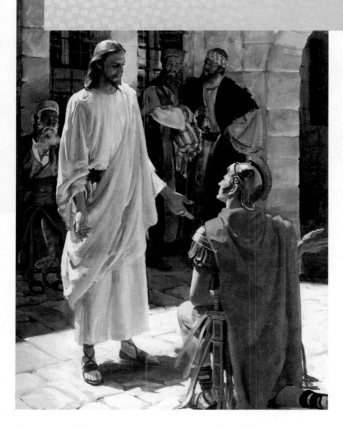

There are four main actions in the celebration of the Sacrament of Penance:

- expressing sorrow for sin, which is known as contrition
- confession of sin to the priest
- doing penance, which means doing something to make up for the damage caused by sin
- absolution, which means a "freeing from guilt" caused by sin. God gives us absolution through the words of the priest.

After hearing our confession, the priest will give a penance. A penance is a prayer or activity that is meant to help us practice charity and to grow in it. After receiving a penance, we are asked to make an Act of Contrition. This act is made in the form of a prayer. In it, we state that we are sorry for our sin(s), most of all because we have offended God, who loves us so much. After we make our Act of Contrition, the priest then absolves us in the name of the Father, the Son, and the Holy Spirit, which reminds us that the priest offers us God's forgiveness.

The Sacrament of Penance strengthens our relationship with God.

The Sacrament of Penance has many important effects. The sacrament

- helps us turn away from sin and draws us closer to God
- restores and strengthens our relationship with the Church
- frees us of some of the effects caused by sin, such as a weakened ability to resist temptation
- saves us from eternal separation from God, if we have committed mortal sin
- gives us spiritual comfort.

Only priests whom the Church has given authority to forgive sins in the name of Christ can hear confession and give absolution.

However, when someone is in danger of death, any priest can give absolution.

Activity

Write a short prayer to thank God for the gift of the Sacrament of Penance. Include at least two of the effects of the sacrament from the list above for which you are thankful.

When we are sick or suffering, we can call on God to heal and strengthen us.

In the **Sacrament of Anointing of the Sick**, God's grace and comfort are given to those who are seriously ill or are suffering. In the sacrament, we ask God to heal us and to strengthen us to endure our suffering.

God always remembers those who are sick and suffering. As Christians, we believe that when we suffer, we can unite our suffering with Jesus' suffering on the Cross. Jesus understands our pain and suffering because he was human, too, and even suffered and died on the Cross.

When people are very sick, they may become anxious and discouraged. In the Sacrament of Anointing of the Sick, Christ comforts them and gives them strength.

Faith Word

Anointing of the Sick
see p. 257

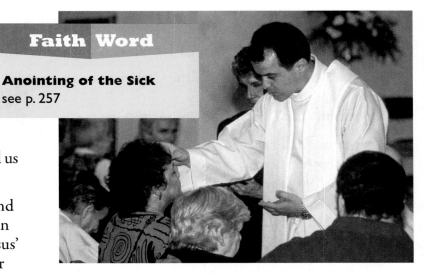

The Sacrament of Anointing of the Sick is sometimes celebrated at Mass.

The Sacrament of Anointing of the Sick helps us see that Christ knows what we are feeling because he suffered, too. It helps us join our suffering to Jesus' own suffering. It gives us peace and courage. It heals us of illness if that is God's will. It forgives our sins.

The Sacrament of Anointing of the Sick is a celebration with the whole community of the faithful. Those present from the parish offer comfort and support to those who are sick. Sometimes the sacrament is celebrated during Mass. More often it is celebrated in hospitals, homes, at the site of an accident, or wherever someone is in danger of death because of illness or old age.

Only a priest or bishop can administer Anointing of the Sick. The sacrament can be celebrated more than once. If people recover after being anointed but become sick at another time, they may receive the sacrament again. When someone is preparing to have surgery, he or she can receive the sacrament with family, friends, and their parish.

One Church, Many Cultures

Pope Benedict XVI said that God can reveal himself "by using languages, imagery and expressions that are bound to different cultures" (*Verbum Domini*, 2010). The Church is made up of many cultures. Yet we may not always reflect an attitude of acceptance and welcome to others. We need to find ways to express healing and reconciliation for the times we have excluded other cultures and people or have been dismissive of them. Pope Francis has asked forgiveness for any harm caused to native peoples, among other groups, especially during the time of early missionary work in the Americas. Today, Native Americans and other diverse groups work within the Church to promote healing and reconciliation.

Activity

Think about those in your parish who are sick. Write a prayer asking God to help them. If possible, do something special for someone who is sick this week. You might call, visit, or email the person, or send a card.

The Sacrament of Anointing of the Sick continues Jesus' mission of healing.

When we care for members of the Church who are sick, we are caring for the Body of Christ. We serve Christ himself.

Out of love for Christ and his Body, we work to help others feel better. We try to provide them with the things they need. We join them in the celebration of the sacraments. These actions are a way to share in Jesus' healing work.

Those who are sick have different needs. Sick children may want us to read to them or play with them. Parents who are ill may need us to perform chores around the house. An elderly person may enjoy a short visit and the chance to talk to someone. Our concern for them is a way to support them on their road to recovery. Using prayer, the whole Church remembers those who are sick, especially when we gather at Sunday Mass.

For those who receive the Sacrament of Anointing of the Sick, it

- renews their trust and faith in God
- unites them to Christ and his suffering
- forgives the person's sins if the person is unable to celebrate the Sacrament of Penance
- prepares them, when necessary, for death and the hope of life forever with God
- may restore them to health.

Activity

Have you ever cared for someone who was sick? What did you do that helped to share in Jesus' mission of healing? What can you share with others to encourage them to help those who are sick or suffering? Write down your thoughts.

_____

_____

_____

Partners in Faith

Sister Rose Hawthorne

Sister Rose was a child of the writer Nathanial Hawthorne. In her early years, she lived in Massachusetts, London, and Rome. Rose had trained as a nurse, and when her husband died in 1898, she decided to devote her life to the care of the sick. Sister Rose Hawthorne's case for sainthood was opened in 2003, and she is now known as a Servant of God.

 Learn more about the life of Sister Rose Hawthorne.

Faith Words

Anointing of the Sick
Penance and Reconciliation
Sacraments of Healing

 ## Show What You Know

In your own words, give a short definition of each part of the Sacrament of Anointing of the Sick. Write your definition on the lines below, or discuss it with a partner.

Prayer of faith

_____

_____

_____

Laying on of hands

_____

_____

_____

Anointing with oil

_____

_____

_____

Live Your Faith

• What are the effects of the Sacrament of Penance?

_____

_____

_____

• Give an example of how you have experienced God's healing in your own life.

_____

_____

_____

Portfolio

How can I help others know God's forgiveness and healing?

Mini-Task

Celebrating the Sacraments of Healing can bring comfort and strength to all who are ill in body, mind, or spirit.

Imagine you are being asked to plan a healing service for your parish. Consider when and where you would hold the service, who will be invited, and ways to let people know about the healing service. Use the chart to guide you.

Healing Service	Planning
Environment	
Music	
Opening Prayer	
Reading from Psalms	
Reading from the Gospel	
Intercessions	
Blessing	

 Want to do more? Go to your Portfolio to continue this activity.

 At Home

Jesus works through his Body, the Church, to bring healing and comfort to the suffering. Your family is part of the Body of Christ. Are there people you know who are suffering? How can your family share Jesus' love with those people, even in small ways, today or tomorrow?

How are we strengthened for service to God and others?

The Sacraments at the Service of Communion give us special grace to serve God and others. In the Sacrament of Holy Orders, the Church calls baptized men to serve the Church by teaching, leading the faithful in worship, and living as disciples of Christ. In the Sacrament of Matrimony, a man and a woman are given the grace to love each other as Christ loves the Church. Together they form a Christian family that is a community of faith, grace, and prayer.

Go to the digital portal for a meditation prayer.

"In happiness may they praise you, O Lord,
in sorrow may they seek you out;
may they have the joy of your presence
to assist them in their toil,
and know that you are near
to comfort them in their need;
let them pray to you in the holy assembly
and bear witness to you in the world."

Roman Missal, Nuptial Blessing

> *"Whoever wishes to be great among you shall be your servant; whoever wishes to be first among you shall be your slave. Just so, the Son of Man did not come to be served but to serve."*
>
> *Matthew 20:26–28*

Faith Words

common priesthood of the faithful see p. 257

Sacraments at the Service of Communion see p. 258

The Sacrament of Baptism calls us to service.

Through Baptism, Confirmation, and the Eucharist, we share a common vocation, or calling, with all of the faithful. We share a call to holiness and to spread the Good News. The Sacraments of Initiation give us the grace we need to share in God's life and in his divine plan to share eternity with him.

When Jesus was baptized, the Holy Spirit marked him as priest, prophet, and king. Our anointing at Baptism makes us sharers in Christ's role as priest, prophet, and king. We share in Christ's priestly mission. This is known as the **common priesthood of the faithful**. In the common priesthood, each of us is called to worship God, spread the Good News of Jesus Christ, and serve others and the Church.

We share in Christ's kingly mission, not a kingship of power *over* others but of service *to* others.

Two other sacraments call those who celebrate them to serve others. Their service helps the

How do I serve others?

Church grow in holiness both through the ministerial priesthood, or ordained ministry, and through married life. Holy Orders and Matrimony are the **Sacraments at the Service of Communion**. They are directed toward the salvation of others.

Did You Know?

The laity are members of the common priesthood of the faithful.

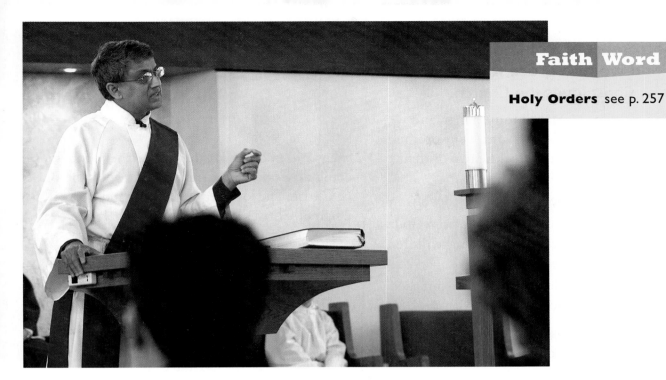

Faith Word

Holy Orders see p. 257

The Sacrament of Holy Orders gives special authority to teach and lead the faithful.

One of the ways that God calls baptized men to serve him through the Church is in the **Sacrament of Holy Orders**. In this sacrament, men are ordained to serve the Church as deacons, priests, and bishops. It is a Sacrament at the Service of Communion. Those who receive the Sacrament of Holy Orders take on a special mission in leading and serving the People of God.

In the Sacrament of Holy Orders, men are ordained by the bishop's laying on of hands and prayer of consecration. Those who are ordained receive the grace that is necessary to carry out their ministry to the faithful. They receive an indelible sacramental character, a permanent spiritual seal on their souls.

The Church, through its ordained ministers, continues the mission that Jesus Christ first gave to his Apostles (see John 20:20–23). Men who are ordained minister in the person of Christ, as head of the Church, and as priest, prophet, and king. Through the grace of the Holy Spirit, they serve the Church by teaching the faithful, leading divine worship, and leading the universal Church.

"The disciples rejoiced when they saw the Lord. [Jesus] said to them again, 'Peace be with you. As the Father has sent me, so I send you.' And when he had said this, he breathed on them and said to them, 'Receive the holy Spirit. Whose sins you forgive are forgiven them, and whose sins you retain are retained.'" John 20:20–23

Activity

Priests and deacons receive the Sacrament of Holy Orders. Write down three questions you'd like to know about what it is like to be either a priest or a deacon.

Share your questions with the group. What do your group's questions tell you about your understanding of the Sacrament of Holy Orders?

_____

_____

_____

_____

The Sacrament of Matrimony gives a man and woman grace to love each other as Christ loves the Church.

Faith Word

Matrimony see p. 258

In the **Sacrament of Matrimony**, a man and woman become husband and wife. They promise to be faithful to each other for the rest of their lives. They

• promise to love and be true to each other always

• lovingly accept their children as a gift from God, not preventing themselves from having children using unacceptable methods

• are strengthened by God's grace to live out their promises to Christ and each other.

The Sacrament of Matrimony is about God first. God calls a man and woman into a sacred covenant. Together they will bring God's love to the world in a way greater than either of them could do alone. The Church is known as the Bride of Christ. The love between a husband and wife is a sign of Christ's love for his Church. It is a love that is generous, faithful, and complete.

The Sacrament of Matrimony gives a married couple the grace

• to bring God's love to the world together

• to live the Paschal Mystery in their marriage together

• to live a life of discipleship together.

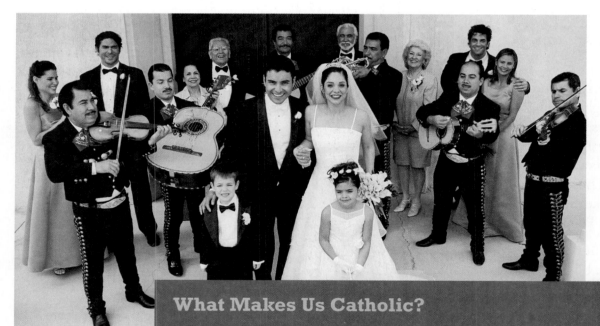

What Makes Us Catholic?

Catholic couples may choose to be married in the same church where the bride or groom was baptized. Before the ceremony, the couple must bring copies of their certificates of Baptism to the church where they will be married. Catholic couples also get ready to celebrate the sacrament by participating in a marriage preparation program through their parish or diocese. This includes spiritual guidance, Church teaching on building a home and family, and instruction on how to complete forms the Church requires.

God created marriage for the good of the married couple and for the good of his Church. Jesus made it into a symbol of his love for us by giving it to the Church as a sacrament. In the marriage covenant between a husband and wife, we see the love of Jesus for the Church. When a man and a woman celebrate the Sacrament of Matrimony, they—not the priest or deacon—are the celebrants of the sacrament. They give themselves to each other.

The love the bride and groom have for each other is blessed and strengthened by the grace of the sacrament. The couple is also blessed by the members of the Church community. The bride and groom together become a sign of God's love to the Church and the world. As husband and wife, the married couple acts as a sign of Christ's presence and saving grace.

One Church, Many Cultures

In the Latin, or Roman, Catholic Church, the married couple are the celebrants, or ministers, of the Sacrament of Matrimony. In the Eastern Catholic Churches, the priest is considered to be the celebrant. In the Eastern Church, some marriage ceremonies also include a "holy crowning" of the bride and groom. During the Mass, the priest prays a blessing and places crowns on their heads to mark the couple as part of the Kingdom of God and as king and queen of their home and family.

The Christian family is a community of faith, grace, and prayer.

God's creation of man and woman was the beginning of the human family. He told the first man and woman to "be fertile and multiply" (Genesis 1:28). In this way God blessed the first man and woman to bring new life into the world. He wanted them to have children and share in his plan for creating the human family.

Married couples express their love through their faithfulness to each other. They also show love by being open to God's gift of children. The Christian family is a community of faith, hope, and charity. It is a sign of the love and unity of the Blessed Trinity.

The family is a community of faith. The family grows in faith when its members learn to be disciples of Jesus and members of the Church. The family grows in faith when it celebrates the sacraments together, especially Sunday Eucharist. Its members grow in faith when they learn and practice Christian virtue.

As a community of grace, the family shares God's life and love among its members and with the community in acts of loving service. It shares God's grace and experiences Jesus' love when family members forgive and are forgiven, and when they take care of one another. The family is also a community of prayer. When a family includes prayer in everyday life, it acknowledges the presence of God in every moment.

Activity

The family is a community of prayer. Choose one of the following events. Write a short prayer for your family to pray at these times. Teach it to your family.

- before homework
- in the car
- before a practice or activity
- after school

Partners in Faith

Saint Thomas More

Saint Thomas More was a lawyer. In 1529, King Henry VIII made him the chancellor of England. He helped the king rule England. Thomas loved his family and made sure that his daughters had the same education as his son. When the king wanted to divorce his wife and marry someone else, Thomas opposed the marriage. King Henry eventually had him beheaded.

 Learn more about the life of Saint Thomas More.

Faith Words

common priesthood of the faithful
Sacraments at the Service of Communion
Holy Orders   Matrimony

☑ Show What You Know

Choose the correct word to complete the sentences.

1. In Matrimony, a _____ man and woman become husband and wife and promise to be faithful to each other for the rest of their lives.

baptized | beatified

2. The sacrament in which baptized men are ordained to serve the Church as deacons, priests, and bishops is called Holy _____.

Communion | Orders

3. The common _____ is Christ's priestly mission in which everyone who has been baptized share.

good | priesthood

Live Your Faith

• What do the two Sacraments at the Service of Communion have in common?

_____
_____
_____
_____
_____
_____

• How do you share in Christ's priestly mission?

_____
_____
_____
_____
_____
_____

How do I share Christ's love through service?

Mini-Task

As Jesus' disciples, we are called to care for those in need. Catholic Relief Services (CRS) is an international organization committed to helping people meet their basic needs. Whether providing access to clean water, healthy food, or education, CRS sends thousands of volunteers to do the work of Christ around the world.

In the space below, write five things you consider basic needs. How can you help provide them for others?

Basic Needs

_____

_____

_____

_____

_____

_____

_____

_____

_____

_____

 Want to do more? Go to your Portfolio to continue this activity.

 At Home

Jesus tells us that he came not to be served but to serve. Over the next week, find a way to serve another person with love, as Jesus serves us. Involve your family in this project.

Unit 3
The Faith Lived

Paul Preaches to Love One Another

Unit Prayer

Leader: Saint Ignatius of Loyola taught that God's reason for creating us is to draw a response of love and service from us on earth. He also believed that all of creation exists for us to know God better and to help us to love and serve him. Let us listen to stories of people among us who have used God's creation to better know, love, and serve him.

Let us listen to stories of missionary disciples among us.

Leader: O God, when we look at our own face, we see your beauty. We praise you for your wonderful works.

All: We praise you for your wonderful works.

Leader: O God, we see you in the faces of everyone you have created.

All: We praise you for your wonderful works.

Leader: O God, you show us how much you love us by the gift of your creation.

All: We praise you for your wonderful works.

Leader: We praise you and show our love for you when we serve each other and care for all your creation.

All: We praise you for your wonderful works.

End the Unit Prayer by singing the song for this unit.

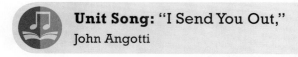

Unit Song: "I Send You Out," John Angotti

Missionary Discipleship

hen were you asked to be of service to someone else? What did you do? How did you feel? Was there a time when someone served you?

How do we know God loves us?

God created us in his image, body and soul. He gave us the gift of free will. Free will allows us to choose what we do. Free will is the basis for our moral responsibility. God's grace helps us use our free will to choose what is morally good and right. The natural law, which God has imprinted in our hearts, is the moral law we are born with. It guides our understanding of what is morally good.

 Go to the digital portal for a meditation prayer.

"Before all else be free persons! Freedom means . . . knowing how to [choose] behaviors that make us grow. . . . it will make you persons with a backbone, who know how to face life, [and live as] courageous and patient persons."

Pope Francis, June 7, 2013

We are created in God's image, with free will and a soul.

God freely chose to enter into a relationship with humanity. And when he did, he created us in his image and likeness. We are his most wonderful creation, because he willed it to be so. He created us with a body and a spiritual soul, with an intellect, and with **free will**.

Each of us is on a journey toward God and eternal happiness with him in heaven. From the moment of our conception, God breathed his life into us, giving us a soul. That we are body and soul, together, is what makes us fully human. Even though our body will one day die, our soul will live on, awaiting the hope of our resurrected body.

God also created each of us with an intellect and free will. These gifts mean we can freely choose to cooperate with God's action in our lives and his plan for us. God invites us to become his adopted children, and he gives us the grace that helps us

Faith Word

free will see p. 257

respond to this invitation. There is nothing we can do on our own to deserve this grace. God's grace is a gift he freely gives to us.

The life of a Christian disciple involves freely choosing to receive the holiness of God and participating in God's divine life. Sometimes we stray from the path and take detours on our journey to God. We freely choose not to cooperate with God's plan. God always takes the first step to bring us back to him.

Jesus' sacrifice on the Cross will forever have the power to draw us back to God the Father and to Jesus. In the sacraments Jesus gave to the Church, we are cleansed from our sins and reconciled with God. Sacraments make us sharers in God's life, love, and work.

What does it mean to have free will?

Did You Know?

 There are many ways to be happy.

Activity

Having free will makes us responsible for our own choices and actions. It means we have the ability to choose what we do or do not do. This does not mean we do whatever we want. God's law requires us to do what is good and to reject what is sinful. God's grace helps us to choose what is good.

Write a story about a young person who is having trouble freely choosing to cooperate with God's plan. Perhaps the young person is being bullied by peers to not choose freely. Write the title of your story below. How does your main character exercise free will?

_____

_____

_____

God's grace helps us respect and care for others and ourselves.

What do you see when you look in a mirror? You see a person created in the image and likeness of God. Now imagine looking in the same mirror and seeing not your face but the faces of the people in your life—family members, classmates, friends, and neighbors. Use your imagination to see the faces of people from all walks of life—young and old, different nationalities, races, and ethnicities—and from all over the world. These people, too, are created in the image and likeness of God.

The Church teaches that each of these people is "another self." This means that in a certain sense we see ourselves in other people, people created in the image and likeness of God, people whom God calls to be one with him. We see people whom God is calling to live forever in happiness with him, just like we are called to live.

When we see ourselves in other people, when we stand in their shoes, we recognize that we all have a fundamental right to be treated with dignity. Every person deserves respect and care.

Faith Word

morality see p. 258

Morality is the goodness or evil of our actions. A good moral life is lived according to the teaching of Jesus and the Church. Every choice or act we make is based on three elements: the *objective* (the object, or what we do); the *intention* (the goal, or why we do the act); and the *situation or circumstance* in which we perform the action (such as where, when, with whom, and how).

What Makes Us Catholic?

God gave all of us human dignity. The Catholic Church teaches us to respect each other's minds, hearts, and bodies. We do this when we speak up for those who are being treated unkindly. Youth groups in some parishes in the United States have formed anti-bullying programs. They spread the word about showing respect for everyone. All Catholic young people are encouraged to stand up for what is right for themselves and for others. We are called to work together to stop bullying and other injustices.

Activity

We are all created in the image of God. One way we honor this is through the Golden Rule: Do to others what you would have them do to you. On the Golden Rule chart below, write one thing that you do for others that you would like them to do for you, using the letters as a guide.

G	
O	
L	
D	
E	
N	
R	
U	
L	
E	

A good moral choice is one in which the object, or goal, of what we are doing and the circumstance of the act are good. The intention behind our actions—why we do the act—also must be good.

However, a good intention never makes a bad or evil action right or good. Some acts are always evil and morally wrong. The end never justifies the means.

In addition, the situation or circumstance within which we make a moral choice can either increase or decrease the goodness of an act. The act, the intention, and the circumstance all have to be good in order to be a morally good act.

The choices we make every day show whether or not we respect and care for ourselves and others. Our actions demonstrate whether or not we truly understand that every person is our neighbor—our brother or sister—in Jesus Christ.

God's grace, poured out on us most especially in the sacraments, helps us to seek the good in each other and ourselves. God's grace helps us respect and care for others and ourselves.

Let us look at an example. Ryan is sitting in class during a test. He knows his friend did not have time to study for this test because he had to take care of his younger sister the night before. Ryan cares about his friend and wants him to do well on the test, so he shares some answers with him when the teacher isn't looking.

Although Ryan's *intentions* are good (to help his friend pass the test), the *act* of cheating is still morally wrong.

Free will is our God-given gift and ability to choose between right and wrong.

God created us as rational beings, each with a soul and intellect, and each with the dignity of being able to choose and control our own actions. The *Catechism of the Catholic Church* tells us that we have the freedom "to act or not to act, to do this or that" (*CCC*, 1731).

"You made me do it!" We have all heard and even said this at one time or another. The fact is, our voluntary actions, or actions that another person is not forcing us to do, are our own responsibility. They are not the responsibility of any other person or group.

Sometimes we don't know the right thing to do. We might act without knowing that what we are doing is not right. Or, there are situations when a person might be acting out of fear. These situations are examples of why it's so important to understand that we have no right to take away another person's freedom.

All people have the right to use their free will to follow God's law. We owe each other this respect as people created in the image of God, with human dignity. We should also note that free will does not mean people have a right to say or do anything they want.

Free will is an amazing and awesome gift God has given us. The choices we make in exercising free will shape our lives. This freedom to be responsible

for our own choices is a tremendous force for good in the world when we direct it toward God, toward happiness with him.

There is always the possibility of choosing between good and evil. When we choose the good, we grow toward the life with God that he desires for us. The more we choose and do what is good, the freer we become. When we choose evil, we sin by failing to love.

By God's grace, we use our free will to choose what is good and right, even when it is difficult for us to do so. The Holy Spirit working within us guides us to choose what is good and just. Most especially, we grow in the proper use of God's gift of free will through participation in the sacraments.

One Church, Many Cultures

Freedom to find opportunities to work and live is a human right. Catholics who are migrants leave their home countries to earn a living so they can support their families. In Ireland, the Catholic Church welcomes migrants from around the world, including Eastern Europe. Migrants from Poland, for example, participate in one of the many Masses celebrated in the Polish language. Some Irish Catholics who are not Polish also attend these Masses. It is a way for them to be welcoming and enjoy the different cultural experience, including Polish liturgical music.

Natural law is the moral law we are born with.

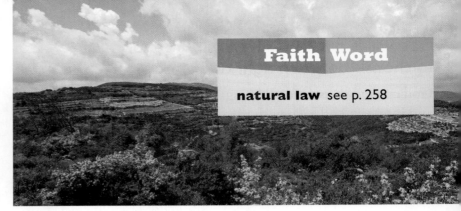

Faith Word

natural law see p. 258

Have you ever wondered where your sense of right and wrong comes from? Every day, we encounter situations about which we can say "That just isn't right!" Or, on the other hand, we can also say "that *is* the right thing to do." Consider a time in which you see a friend being bullied. You might think: "That's not right!" And, with courage, you might do what you know *is* right and stand up for your friend.

This sense of right and wrong is based on **natural law**, our God-given desire to be in right relationship with him, others, and ourselves. The natural law is the moral law we are born with. It is placed in our hearts by God and is part of human nature. Natural law directs us to naturally seek God and follow a path where we choose what is good for us and for others.

We have this natural understanding of what is morally good because we are created in God's image. We have the use of reason and common sense. Natural law helps us discover, using reason, the way to true happiness. At the same time, it helps us recognize that which turns us away from God, that which is evil. Natural law expresses the dignity of the human person. It is the guide for how we live as God's images in the world. It is the basis for our fundamental rights and duties as people.

God's saving plan was fulfilled in Christ's life, suffering, Death, and Resurrection. In him, a new and everlasting covenant was made. To show us how to live as members of this new covenant, Jesus said to his disciples: "Do to others whatever you would have them do to you. This is the law and the prophets" (Matthew 7:12).

Like the disciples, we look to Christ, who calls us to live by this Golden Rule, a New Law that perfects the Old Law established in the Ten Commandments. In the Sermon on the Mount, Jesus teaches us about the New Law: love our enemies, be peacemakers, live humbly, pray, trust in God. The grace of the Holy Spirit urges us to act out of love. The Sermon on the Mount teaches us what to do, and the sacraments give us the grace to do it.

Partners in Faith

Saint Thomas Aquinas

Saint Thomas Aquinas is one of the greatest theologians and philosophers of the Church. Thomas was a Dominican priest. His work *Summa Theologiae* is still studied in universities and seminaries today. One of his greatest contributions is his explanation of natural law. Near the end of his life, he experienced a mystical vision that caused him to stop writing and spend more time in prayer.

 Learn more about the life of Saint Thomas Aquinas.

Faith Words

free will

morality   natural law

 ## Show What You Know

Answer the questions.

1. What do we call the moral law we are born with that God placed in our hearts?

_____

2. What term describes how we determine the goodness or evil of what we do or how we behave in situations?

_____

3. What do we call God's gift of the freedom and ability to choose to cooperate with his plan for us?

_____

Live Your Faith

• When have you used your free will to show that you are following God's will for you?

_____

_____

_____

_____

_____

_____

• What helps you to determine the morality of an action, a decision, or a choice?

_____

_____

_____

_____

_____

_____

Mini-Task

We have the ability to choose to follow Christ or to stray from his teachings. Developing a strong moral compass means that we know right from wrong, exercise our freedom, and choose to do good. A compass always guides the way. Read the following situation. Then fill in the compass below with choices that show movement toward Christ (north), away from Christ (south), or decisions that are somewhere in between (east and west).

A friend wants to attend a concert. His parents have told him he cannot go. He asks you to pretend that he is spending the night at your house while he actually goes to the concert instead. What are some choices and decisions you can make?

 Want to do more? Go to your Portfolio to continue this activity.

At Home

Every person in your family was created in the image and likeness of God. Share with each other how you see the image of God in each of your family members.

How do we respond to God's love?

God has placed the desire for happiness in every human heart. As we come to know who God is and seek happiness with him, we use an informed conscience to make good choices. We are guided by God, Scripture, and Church teaching. The divine grace of the sacraments strengthens us to live a virtuous life and work for peace, justice, and the common good.

Go to the digital portal for a prayer of thanksgiving.

"Above all, let your love for one another be intense, because love covers a multitude of sins."

1 Peter 4:8

What leads me to God?

God has placed the desire for happiness in every human heart.

Saint Thomas Aquinas wrote: "God alone satisfies" (see *Catechism of the Catholic Church*, 1718). God's divine image is present in each of us. God created us out of love and for love. For this purpose, he created us with a longing for him, with a law written on our hearts and minds that guides us in discovering how to love as he loves.

God's plan for us, from the moment of conception, is that we share eternal beatitude, or happiness with him forever. Through our belief in Jesus Christ, we become sons and daughters of God, and we have new life in the Holy Spirit. The Holy Spirit makes present the action of God's grace in our lives, especially through the sacraments. The Holy Spirit directs us toward love of God and love of neighbor. We seek and love what is true and good. We advance toward the glory of heaven, where God has always intended us to be.

The Beatitudes (see Matthew 5:3–12), which are at the heart of Jesus' teachings, reveal the goal of human existence: to share in God's life and beatitude, or happiness, forever. They provide a path for us to follow. God invites us to follow this path that leads to the Kingdom of God.

One Church, Many Cultures

God plants certain virtues in our hearts. These virtues guide Catholic laypeople around the world to carry out Christ's mission. For example, the Sant'Egidio community extends the hand of friendship to people everywhere, especially people in need. Based in Rome, the community was founded by a high school student named Andrea Riccardi in 1968. Since then, it has spread to over seventy countries. Sant'Egidio members dedicate themselves to a life of service and prayer and bringing peace to the world.

Activity

Think about a time when you got something you really wanted, but you were not as happy about it as you thought you would be. Share your experience with a friend. Now talk about a time when you felt God's love and how that made you feel. Share your feelings with a larger group.

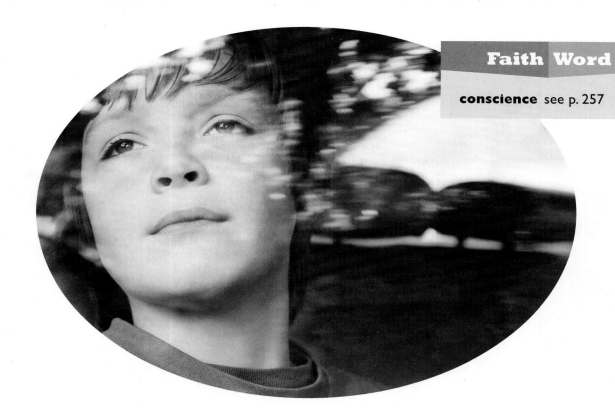

Faith Word

conscience see p. 257

An informed conscience is formed and guided by God, human reason, and Church teachings.

Every person is called to follow natural law, the law that God has imprinted on our hearts. Our **conscience** is a God-given "interior voice" that enables us to know what is morally right or wrong. Our conscience guides us in following natural law. This gift from God helps us understand that we are responsible for our actions. It urges us to make good moral decisions and to avoid evil.

Every day we face situations in which we can either choose to do good or choose to do bad, or evil. We can make choices that reflect God's love and law, or we can make choices that don't. Educating our conscience about what is right and what is wrong is a lifelong task. An informed, well-educated conscience helps us make good choices about our words and actions.

God guides us in hearing the voice of our conscience to make life-giving choices.

God created us with the ability to follow his plan for us. God also created us with the ability to reason. Reason guides our conscience to make the right judgments. With the gift of reason, we have the ability to recognize whether or not a concrete action is good or evil. We also turn to the teachings of the Church, both in Sacred Scripture and Sacred Tradition, to inform our conscience in all that is true and good.

When we examine our conscience, such as when we celebrate the Sacrament of Penance and Reconciliation, we do so in light of God's truth, reason, and Church teaching. We determine whether the choices we have made showed love for God, ourselves, and others. We ask the Holy Spirit to help us judge the goodness of our thoughts, words, and actions.

Did You Know?

 All people long for happiness.

Faith Word

virtue see p. 259

The divine grace of the sacraments strengthens us to live a virtuous life.

Good habits are a good thing. Good habits can help us be happy, healthy, and holy people. The Church recognizes the value in having good habits. Good spiritual habits called **virtues** help us to act according to God's plan for us. People who are virtuous make these habits or virtues a part of their lives. People who are virtuous are people who *practice* or live the virtues in their concrete actions. They are in the habit of choosing and doing good.

What is the point of living a virtuous life? The *Catechism* tells us that living a virtuous life "allows the person not only to perform good acts, but to give the best of himself" (*CCC*, 1803).

Every day, Christ calls us to follow him and live by his teachings. Every day, we have the opportunity to act as Jesus' disciples. The choices we make show whether or not we follow Jesus' example. Sometimes we do not even realize that we are making a choice. We show love and respect because we are in the habit of doing it. We are living a life of virtue.

What Makes Us Catholic?

The Church's sacraments help us to respond to God's grace and grow in virtue. They strengthen us to share God's love with the world. For example, the Sacrament of Confirmation strengthens the gifts of the Holy Spirit within us to "spread and defend the faith by word and action" (CCC, 1303). The Eucharist "strengthens our charity, which tends to be weakened in daily life" (CCC, 1394). Celebrating the sacraments boosts our ability to give the best of ourselves—to live virtuous lives.

The virtues lead us to know and love God and to work for the common good.

God's grace, which we receive in the sacraments, helps us to live virtuous lives. For example, in the Sacrament of Baptism, we celebrate the gift and virtue of faith. Faith in God guides us all throughout our lives: "Behold, I am with you always, until the end of the age" (Matthew 28:20).

The **Theological Virtues** of faith, hope, and charity are gifts from God that enable us to live in a relationship with the Holy Trinity. God is their origin, their motive, and their object.

- Faith helps us know God and believe in all he has revealed. It helps us respond to God's invitation to believe in him and love him.
- Hope keeps us focused on the promise of eternal life with God. It helps us trust in God and his promises.
- Charity, or love, helps us care for others and work to meet their needs out of love for God and others. Love is the beginning and end of Christian life.

The moral or **Cardinal Virtues** are habits that come about by our own efforts. The Cardinal Virtues are the virtues of prudence, justice, fortitude, and temperance.

Faith Words

Theological Virtues see p. 259
Cardinal Virtues see p. 257

The Cardinal Virtues are brought to life by the Theological Virtues. Yet we have to work to acquire the Cardinal Virtues and work to keep them! We have to learn about them, practice them, and keep practicing them.

The Cardinal Virtues guide the way we think, feel, and behave. They lead us to live a good life. They result from our making the decision, over and over again, to live by God's law.

While it does take a lot of our own effort to develop these virtues, we are not left on our own to struggle. For one thing, when we receive the gifts of the Holy Spirit, they also help us live virtuous lives. These seven gifts—wisdom, understanding, counsel, fortitude, knowledge, piety, and fear of the Lord—perfect the virtues. Most especially, God's divine grace—available to us in the sacraments—helps us develop these virtues and gifts of the Spirit so that they grow in us over time.

Our vocation, or calling from God, is "to show forth the image of God and to be transformed into the image of the Father's only Son" (*CCC*, 1877). This is our vocation as individuals, and it is our vocation as a human community. So what does it mean for how we are to live?

prudence	helps us to use reason to find the true good in every situation
justice	helps us to respect others and give them what is rightfully theirs
fortitude	helps us to use strength or courage to use good judgment and behavior during difficult or challenging times
temperance	helps us to use earthly goods in moderation

Activity

Write another word for each virtue. List one way that you can work on each.

prudence: _____

justice: _____

temperance: _____

fortitude: _____

Faith Words

society see p. 259

solidarity see p. 259

First, we cannot love God and hate our neighbor. It just isn't possible. We need to live with each other in mutual love and service. In this way, we develop our potential and respond to God's call to be his image in the world. **Society** is a group of people bound together by a principle of unity that goes beyond any one individual. A society works for the common good, social conditions that allow all people to meet basic needs and achieve fulfillment. A society has a spiritual purpose—to fulfill the human vocation.

Society must promote the exercise of virtue. One of these virtues is **solidarity**. The Christian is called to consider members of society as people with rights, responsibilities, and fundamental human dignity and also to recognize them as the living images of God. This has a profound impact on our actions, not only in the smaller societies of our families and neighborhoods but also in the world. Saint John Paul II reminds us that each person is called to love his or her enemies "with the same love with which the Lord loves him or her" (*Sollicitudo Rei Socialis*, The Social Concern of the Church, 1987). Every person has worth in God's eyes, and we are made for communion with each other and to share in the life of the Blessed Trinity.

Our actions of solidarity are actions that work for peace, justice, and the common good. These actions aren't optional. They are what is expected of us as humans and as Christians. They are signposts along the way toward salvation and the fulfillment of our vocation to show the image of God.

Partners in Faith

Saint Madeleine Sophie Barat

Saint Madeleine's brother taught her Latin, Greek, science, history, and literature in a time when few girls were educated. She believed that education was a matter of social justice and the common good, and should not be limited to the wealthy. Madeleine also made up her mind that both boys and girls should be educated. She founded many schools throughout Europe.

 Learn more about the life of Saint Madeleine Sophie Barat.

Faith Words

conscience   virtue   Cardinal Virtues
Theological Virtues   society   solidarity

 Show What You Know

Circle the correct answer.

1. Which term means a group of people bound together by a principle of unity that goes beyond any one individual, with a spiritual purpose to fulfill the human vocation?
   a. society
   b. solidarity
   c. sacristy

2. What is a good habit that helps us act according to God's love for us?
   a. vice
   b. virtue
   c. viaticum

3. What word describes our God-given "interior voice" that enables us to know what is morally right and wrong?
   a. consciousness
   b. contrition
   c. conscience

4. What are the Theological Virtues?
   a. justice, fortitude, and fear of the Lord
   b. faith, hope, and charity
   c. temperance, modesty, and piety

Live Your Faith

• How do you show solidarity with others?

_____

_____

_____

_____

• Which of the Cardinal Virtues gives you the most strength?

_____

_____

_____

_____

Mini-Task

The Cardinal Virtues help us to live a happy, holy life. Prudence, justice, temperance, and fortitude guide our relationships with friends and family in real life as well as in the digital world.

Being a good digital citizen means using what you see and read online in a positive way. It means using the Internet to learn about and share what is good, interesting, and helpful, not to create a negative space.

What does being a good digital citizen mean to you? Talk about it with your group. Using the four Cardinal Virtues, plan a design of your own Digital Citizenship poster. Using words and art, give examples for how the virtues will guide your online choices and interactions.

 Want to do more? Go to your Portfolio to continue this activity.

Talk with your family about what a society based on God's law and love for all people would look like. What can your family contribute to that society?

How does God teach us to love?

The Ten Commandments and Church law guide us in knowing, loving, and serving God. The commandments strengthen our relationship with God and guide us to live in truth and love. God's grace helps us keep his laws. By following the Precepts of the Church, we grow and develop as disciples of Jesus.

Go to the digital portal for a prayer of petition.

"Teach me, LORD, your way
that I may walk in your truth,
single-hearted and revering your name."

Psalm 86:11

God's grace helps us to keep his laws.

We all are familiar with rules. Our families have them, our teachers have them, and our communities have them. Rules guide our actions. They tell us what is acceptable and what is not. Have you ever had a hard time following the rules? Sometimes it is difficult, and sometimes we just do not want to.

> "Behold, the days are coming, says the Lord,
>   when I will conclude a new covenant
>   with the house of Israel and the house of
>   Judah. . . .
>
> I will put my laws in their minds
>   and I will write them upon their hearts.
>
> I will be their God,
>   and they shall be my people."
>
> Hebrews 8:8, 10

Who is the ultimate authority for what is right, good, and true? God is. Each of us is called to live in happiness with God. This is God's desire for us and the desire of every human heart. However, wounded by sin, we sometimes lose our way. We are a people who stand in need of God's saving grace. The moral law—revealed by God in the Ten Commandments and fulfilled by Christ in the New Law, or Law of the Gospel—shows us the way to achieve eternal beatitude, happiness with God.

1 Corinthians 13:4–8

The New Law, or law of love, is the work of Jesus Christ. It is the grace of the Holy Spirit given to us through faith in Christ. In the Sermon on the Mount (see Matthew 5–7), Christ taught us a way of living, a law of love for God, self, and neighbor. Saint Augustine tells us that Christ's law of love gives us "the perfect way of the Christian life. . . . This sermon contains . . . all the precepts needed to shape one's life" (CCC, 1966). We discover the qualities and actions of people blessed by God. Through the sacraments, God gives us the grace to follow the New Law and live as happy people.

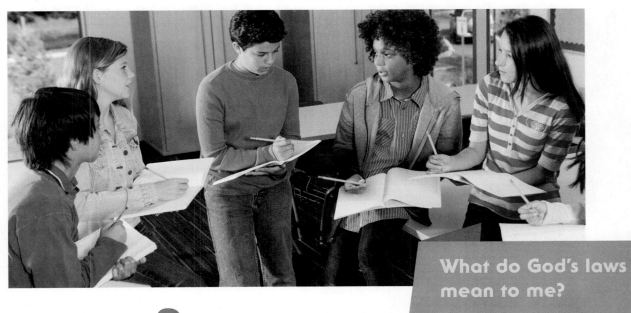

What do God's laws mean to me?

Did You Know?

God gives us laws out of love.

The Ten Commandments strengthen our relationship with God.

God's purpose in giving us the Ten Commandments was to teach us how to live in right relationship with him. We grow closer to God when we follow them. The Ten Commandments strengthen our relationship with him. God gives us the grace we need to follow his commandments.

In the First Commandment, God said:

"I am the LORD your God, who brought you out of the land of Egypt, out of the house of slavery. You shall not have other gods beside me" (Exodus 20:2–3).

We are called to believe in God, hope in him, and love him above all else. We are called to manifest, or show forth to the world, the one true God in whose image we are created. We celebrate the presence of God in the sacraments, most especially in the Sacrament of the Eucharist. Sacramentals, such as sacred objects and images, draw our attention to the one true God. They help us honor God and deepen our relationship with him.

In the Second Commandment, God said:

"You shall not invoke the name of the LORD, your God, in vain. For the LORD will not leave unpunished anyone who invokes his name in vain" (Exodus 20:7).

One Church, Many Cultures

Sacramentals can help us focus our attention on God and his love for us. In Uganda, Catholics celebrate their faith in special ways using sacramentals that include holy water and religious images. At the shrine of Our Lady Queen of Peace at Kiwamirembe, Catholics use sacramentals in their devotions. Statues on the mountain at the shrine depict different Mysteries of the Rosary and the Stations of the Cross. Ugandan Catholics also pray the Rosary in hopes of peace in their country.

Activity

The name of God is holy. That is why we should not use God's name in anger or to express surprise. Using God's name in vain means that what we say is not meant to be positive or respectful toward God. Using God's name in vain is against the Second Commandment. Role-play with a friend what you could say to someone who was using God's name in vain. What could you say to someone who believes that using God's name in vain is okay?

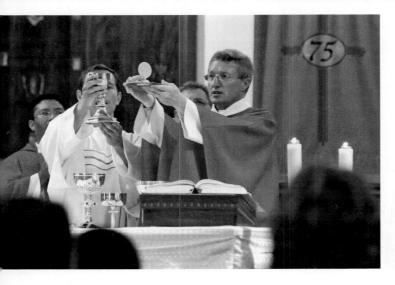

Faith Word

Chosen People see p. 257

Respect for God's name is an expression of respect for God himself. The name of God is holy. The Church begins her prayers and liturgy with the Sign of the Cross: "In the name of the Father and of the Son and of the Holy Spirit. Amen" (*CCC*, 2157). In the Sacrament of Baptism, we are baptized "in the name of the Father, and of the Son, and of the Holy Spirit."

In the Third Commandment, God said:

"Remember the sabbath day—keep it holy. Six days you may labor and do all your work, but the seventh day is a sabbath of the LORD your God. You shall not do any work, . . . For in six days the LORD made the heavens and the earth, the sea and all that is in them; but on the seventh day he rested. That is why the LORD has blessed the sabbath day and made it holy" (Exodus 20:8–11).

God's **Chosen People** were the Israelites, whom God chose to be his people, and he would be their God. For them, the Sabbath was to be a day for the Lord, holy and set apart to praise God, his work of creation, and his saving action in their lives. Sunday, the Lord's Day, is the Christian fulfillment of the Sabbath. Sunday Mass is at the heart of our Catholic celebration of the Lord's Day. We celebrate the Paschal Mystery—the Passion, Death, Resurrection, and Ascension of Jesus—and we worship and adore God, present in the most profound way in the Eucharist. The Lord's Day is so important to our own lives and the life of the Church that the Church requires us to participate in Mass on Sundays and on Holy Days of Obligation. Sunday is a holy day, a day of joy and grace.

God calls us to adore him and only him. Adoration of God is an action of worship, an acknowledgment of God as Creator and Savior, the Lord and Master of everything that exists. Without God, we cannot exist. We adore and bless God in the Church's liturgy, most especially on Sunday, the Lord's Day.

What Makes Us Catholic?

To trace the roots of the Catholic faith, we look to our Old Testament ancestors in faith, the Chosen People. The tradition of the Jewish Sabbath continues in our celebration of Sunday as the Lord's Day. In the evening Mass on Holy Thursday, we read the story of the Passover meal celebrated when God led the Israelites out of Egypt. It was during a Passover meal that Jesus celebrated the Eucharist with his disciples. Our celebration of Pentecost is also connected to a Jewish feast called Shavuot, which occurs forty days after Passover. The Holy Spirit came upon Jesus' Apostles during the festival of Shavuot in Jerusalem, and the Church's public ministry began.

The Ten Commandments guide us to live in truth and love.

Jesus had a special gift of helping his followers focus on what was most important. He summarized the Old Law with the New Law, the Law of Love:

"You shall love the Lord, your God, with all your heart, with all your soul, and with all your mind. This is the greatest and the first commandment. The second is like it: You shall love your neighbor as yourself" (Matthew 22:37–39).

We draw strength to love our neighbor from the Eucharist: the new covenant Christ made in his Body and Blood.

The Ten Commandments are a "how-to" guide for right relationships. Take a closer look at how the Fourth through Tenth Commandments can guide us in our love of neighbor.

Fourth Commandment: "Honor your father and your mother" (Exodus 20:12).

- Our parents have authority over us for our own good. We are called to show them respect and to obey them.
- Our parents are entrusted with teaching us about God and our faith.

Fifth Commandment: "You shall not kill" (Exodus 20:13).

- Respect all life, from conception to natural death.
- Protect the poor and vulnerable.
- Avoid actions that bring harm to others.
- Be a peacemaker.

Sixth Commandment: "You shall not commit adultery" (Exodus 20:14).

- Honor the marriage commitment between a husband and wife.
- Practice modesty, which means respecting your body and the bodies of others.
- Practice chastity, which means expressing friendship and love in appropriate ways.

Seventh Commandment: "You shall not steal" (Exodus 20:15).

- Do not cheat or steal.
- Treat people with justice and mercy.
- Be a good steward of God's gifts; use the gifts of creation wisely.

Eighth Commandment: "You shall not bear false witness against your neighbor" (Exodus 20:16).

- Be honest; do not lie.
- Respect the reputation and good name of others.
- Say you are sorry.

Ninth Commandment: "You shall not covet your neighbor's wife" (Exodus 20:17).

- Honor the love between husband and wife.
- Keep your own heart pure. Act with love.
- Be faithful and trustworthy.
- Practice the virtue of temperance, or moderation.
- Do not desire another's spouse.

Tenth Commandment: "You shall not covet your neighbor's house . . . or anything that belongs to your neighbor" (Exodus 20:17).

- Be grateful for God's gifts; do not be jealous of others' gifts.
- Share your material gifts and talents for the benefit of others.

Activity

The Seventh Commandment tells us to be a good stewards of God's gifts. This means taking care of the things we have and taking care of God's creation. What is something you can do to take care of creation each day? Write it below.

_____

_____

The Precepts of the Church strengthen our bond with God and his Church.

Faith Word

Precepts of the Church
see p. 258

The Christian fulfills his or her vocation in the Church, in communion with all the baptized. We receive the Word of God and the New Law of Christ: love of God and love of neighbor. In the liturgy and sacraments, the grace of Christ enlightens and nourishes the Christian life. The moral life—striving for right relationship with God and others—finds its source and summit in the Eucharist.

The pope and bishops have established some laws to help us know and fulfill our responsibilities as members of the Church. The **Precepts of the Church** are positive laws that present the minimum of what a Catholic should do in order to grow in love of God and neighbor. These laws remind us that we are called to grow in holiness and serve the Church. They help us to know and fulfill our responsibilities as members of the Church and to unite us as followers of Jesus Christ. They guide our behavior and teach us how we should act as members of the Church.

Following the Precepts of the Church helps us grow and develop as disciples of Jesus. The precepts also make sure that the Church grows in love for God and neighbor.

1. You shall attend Mass on Sundays and Holy Days of Obligation and rest from servile work.

2. You shall confess your sins at least once a year.

3. You shall receive the Sacrament of the Eucharist at least once during the Easter season.

4. You shall observe the days of fasting and abstinence determined by the Church.

5. You shall help to provide for the needs of the Church.

The Precepts of the Church guide us in how we should act as members of the Church. We also have a duty as citizens to work within our civic communities to contribute to the good of society in a spirit of truth, justice, solidarity, and freedom.

Partners in Faith

Saint Rose of Lima

Saint Rose wanted to show her love for God. She spent many hours in prayer and decided never to marry. For her, the commandments were a way of life. She did penance and fasted every day. She also did needlework and grew flowers to support her family.

 Learn more about the life of Saint Rose of Lima.

Faith Words

Chosen People   **Precepts of the Church**

✓ Show What You Know

In your own words, write definitions for the terms.

Precepts of the Church

_____

_____

_____

_____

_____

Chosen People

_____

_____

_____

_____

_____

Live Your Faith

• Which Precepts of the Church do you find easiest to follow?

_____

_____

_____

_____

_____

• How would you explain the Paschal Mystery to someone who was not Catholic?

_____

_____

_____

_____

_____

_____

How do I live in God's love?

Mini-Task

Choose one of the Ten Commandments or one of the Precepts of the Church from this lesson. Write it below.

_____

_____

What does this law tell us about God's love?

_____

_____

_____

How does following this law show love for God?

_____

_____

_____

How does this law lead to happiness?

_____

_____

_____

What would the effect be of not having this law?

_____

_____

_____

Want to do more? Go to your Portfolio to continue this activity.

At Home

How can your family commit to following the first three of the Ten commandments more closely?

God loves us, and God wants us to return his love. Sin sometimes stands in the way of our loving God and neighbor. Original Sin created in us an inclination toward sin. Sin goes against our human reason and God's love. It damages our relationship with God. Committing sins repeatedly leads to vices, or capital sins, yet God always loves us and forgives us when we are sorry. His grace helps us return to the path of holiness.

Go to the digital portal for a prayer of petition.

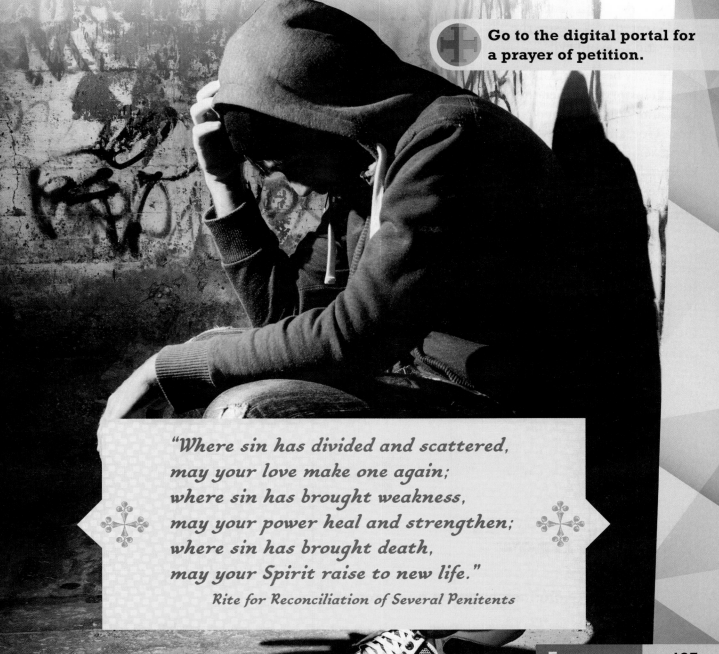

*"Where sin has divided and scattered,
may your love make one again;
where sin has brought weakness,
may your power heal and strengthen;
where sin has brought death,
may your Spirit raise to new life."*

Rite for Reconciliation of Several Penitents

Because of Original Sin, we have an inclination to sin.

God's plan for us includes letting him guide every moment of our lives. This is a life of divine love and human solidarity. God created us in his image and likeness to share in his divine life. God created us to know him, to love him, and to serve him in this life and be happy with him forever in the next. Through grace and the gift of reason, we are able to follow the natural law, which God imprinted on our hearts. We are able to choose what is true and good. God created us to desire the good and to avoid evil.

At the very beginning of our human history, however, the first man and woman turned away from God and disobeyed him. Because of their sin, called Original Sin, they lost their closeness with God, their original holiness and justice. Their love for each other and God became tainted with fear and jealousy. Pride, ignorance, suffering, and death entered the world through the first sin.

Other than Jesus and Mary, everyone is born with Original

Sin, and we suffer its effect throughout our lives. For example, while we may know and want what is good, we are often tempted to turn away from God and commit personal sin.

By his Death and Resurrection, Jesus Christ—the Son of God—saves us from sin. His victory over sin and death offers us salvation.

Where do I see the effects of sin in the world?

Did You Know?

We make choices between good and evil.

Sin goes against our human reason and God's love.

People choose from a variety of operating systems when they buy a computer, smartphone, tablet, or gaming system. The operating system, or OS, supports the device's basic functions. It is the most important program that runs the device.

Humans are not computers, but we can use the comparison to understand something about ourselves: God created us with an awesome "operating system." We are hardwired to love. God created us with all the software and hardware necessary to seek and love all that is true and good. He created us in his image: with a soul, with the ability to reason, and with free will.

Faith Word

sin see p. 259

Sin, however, is like the malware or virus that infects our operating system and causes it to malfunction. And like a virus, sin spreads beyond ourselves. Sin is an offense against God. When we sin, we turn our hearts away from God's love and choose that which we know is wrong. The choices we make weaken God's life in us. Sin is a thought, word, or deed—or a failure to do what we ought—against God's law. Every sin weakens our friendship with God and others.

Activity

Has anyone ever said something about you that was not true? People who do not know you might have believed it. Your reputation might have been hurt by one untrue comment. Work in groups of three to have a panel discussion about a time when someone might have said or shared something that hurt another person. Have the rest of your group ask questions about what could have been done differently.

Sin damages our relationship with God.

When Pope Francis visited the St. Magdalene of Canossa parish in Rome in 2017, a young girl named Sara asked the pope what frightened him. Pope Francis responded that what frightened him was wickedness, the seeds of which can be found in all people. He told the children that the "seeds of wickedness" lie within each human being. What is really frightening, the pope shared, is the harm that people cause by choosing to sin.

At Mass that day, Pope Francis described sin as "a slap" to God's face. Sin is a failure to love God and our neighbor. Sometimes people turn completely away from God's love. They commit very serious sin that breaks their friendship with God. This sin is called **mortal sin**. Those who commit mortal sin must freely choose to do something that they know is seriously wrong. However, God never stops loving people who sin seriously. The Holy Spirit calls them to conversion, to turn back to God.

Faith Word

mortal sin see p. 258

What Makes Us Catholic?

We all have fears. Fear is a real thing and can get in the way of our faith if we give in to it. In Scripture, God often tells us not to be afraid. We are to trust in God and in his love for us. This human fear is different from the "fear of the Lord." This is one of the gifts of the Holy Spirit. It fills us with wonder and awe of God, who created us out of love. It also means putting ourselves in God's hands. Having the "fear of the Lord" puts us in the right relationship with God.

Less serious sin that weakens our friendship with God is called **venial sin**. Even though venial sins do not turn us completely away from God, they still harm our relationship with him, others, and the Church. If we keep repeating them, they can lead us further away from God and the Church. However, God offers us forgiveness when we think or do things that harm our friendship with him or with others.

Faith Word

venial sin see p. 259

We restore our relationship with God in the Sacrament of Penance and Reconciliation. Pope Francis said at the same Mass in 2017: "May [contemplation of Jesus] encourage us to ask forgiveness for our sins, not to sin so much. . . . May it encourage us above all to have faith . . . And he is always willing to forgive us. We need only to ask for it."

One Church, Many Cultures

We can see the "face" of Jesus through the eyes of many artists. Artists often portray Jesus as part of their own culture. The different faces of Jesus remind us that Jesus came to save all people. Artists in Europe often painted Jesus as fair-skinned with light hair, while we know Jesus would have had darker features and hair. Asian and African Christian artists often show Jesus, the Holy Family, and early Christians with features similar to theirs. Seeing different images of Jesus helps us relate to Jesus in a way that is meaningful to us. It helps us to recognize Jesus in ourselves, and it can inspire the way we share Jesus' love and follow his teachings.

 Act of Contrition

Partners in Faith

Saint Magdalene of Canossa

As a teenager, Saint Magdalene of Canossa wanted to be a nun. That was not God's will for her life at the time. Instead, she used her family's fortune to help the poor. Later in her life, she founded a religious order that cared for poor children and worked in hospitals.

 Learn more about the life of Saint Magdalene of Canossa.

Committing sins repeatedly leads to vices, or capital sins.

Over time, people develop habits. Our habits can be either good habits or bad habits. The more often we do something, such as brush our teeth every morning, say grace before meals, or bite our fingernails, the more likely we are to continue doing it.

Committing sin over and over again can become a habit. It reproduces itself and clouds our judgment between what is good and evil. Committing the same sin over and over leads us to form bad habits called **vices**. Vices are the opposite of virtues: they make it easier to sin. They can become deadly sins called capital sins. **Capital sins** separate us from God and from others.

Because of the effects of Original Sin, we are susceptible to the seven capital sins. God's grace helps us stay on the path to holiness, especially through the Sacraments of Eucharist and Penance and Reconciliation, by keeping the commandments, and by practicing the virtues.

Faith Words

vice see p. 259

capital sins see p. 257

Activity

The more we do something, the easier it becomes to do it. That thing becomes a habit. This is true for both good and bad things. Fill in the chart with some things you could do every day to fight against the capital sins. What are some things you could do every day to create a good habit of prayer?

The Seven Capital Sins	Every day, I could . . .
Pride: improper appreciation of one's own worth	
Greed: a sin of excess; desire for earthly goods and power	
Gluttony: eating or drinking too much	
Lust: impure desires of a sexual nature	
Sloth: laziness	
Envy: jealousy; distress over the good fortune of someone else	
Wrath: desire for vengeance, rage, or anger	

Faith Words

| sin | mortal sin |
| venial sin | vice | capital sins |

 Show What You Know

Read the statements. Circle whether the statement is True or False. Correct any false statements you find.

1. Capital sins are the seven "deadly" sins.

(True) | (False)

_____
_____

2. Mortal sin damages but does not break our friendship with God.

True | (False)

_____
_____
_____
_____

3. Although venial sins do not turn us completely away from God, they harm our relationship with him, others, and the Church.

(True) | False

_____
_____

Live Your Faith

• Sin is like a virus. How do you keep the virus of sin from affecting your personal "operating system"?

BY making good desicions and confess
Your sins

• What good habits help you avoid the bad habits that can lead to vices?

confessing atleast once a year.

Why is forgiveness important when I turn away from God?

Mini-Task

Sin harms our relationship with others and with God. While God is always ready to forgive us when we have a contrite heart, it is important to reflect on our actions and ask forgiveness. This is the first step in the Sacrament of Reconciliation. It is also the first step when we seek forgiveness from another person. In the space below, plan a personal narrative about an experience of asking someone for forgiveness.

Forgiveness

What happened?

_____

From whom did you need to ask forgiveness, and why?

_____

_____

How did you ask for forgiveness?

_____

Did the person forgive you?

_____

How did it feel to ask to be forgiven?

_____

_____

Think about and discuss with a partner your answers to the question: How does it feel to forgive others?

 Want to do more? Go to your Portfolio to continue this activity.

At Home

With others in your family, talk about how you can help each other make good choices and resist sin. This week, try to encourage another person in your family who is making good choices.

What turns us toward God's love?

God helps us turn away from sin toward his love. Through God's grace, we share in the life of the Trinity. The Holy Spirit fills our hearts with sanctifying grace. Through Baptism and faith, we are restored to holiness and receive the gift of justification.

Go to the digital portal for a *Lectio* and *Visio Divina* prayer.

"Therefore, since we have been justified by faith, we have peace with God through our Lord Jesus Christ."

Romans 5:1

God helps us turn away from sin and toward his love.

Jesus told the following parable to help us understand what it means to be sorry for our actions and to turn back to God. He explained that a son once asked his father to give him the share of the family's estate that would belong to him. The father did so, but the son soon wasted the money his father had given him. He chose to live a sinful life. The son soon found out that there were consequences to his choice. Jesus said:

"Coming to his senses he thought, 'How many of my father's hired workers have more than enough food to eat, but here am I, dying from hunger. I shall get up and go to my father and I shall say to him, "Father, I have sinned against heaven and against you. I no longer deserve to be called your son; treat me as you would treat one of your hired workers."' So he got up and went back to his father. While he was still a long way off, his father caught sight of him, and was filled with compassion. He ran to his son, embraced him and kissed him. His son said to him, 'Father, I have sinned against heaven and against you; I no longer deserve to be called your son.' But his father ordered his servants, 'Quickly bring the finest robe and put it on him; put a ring on his finger and sandals on his feet. Take the fattened calf and slaughter it. Then let us celebrate with a feast, because this son of mine was dead, and has come to life again; he was lost, and has been found'" (Luke 15:17–24).

God is like the forgiving father in this story. He welcomes us back when we have sinned and rejoices when we decide to turn back to him.

God constantly calls us to **conversion**. Conversion is a turning to God with all one's heart. If we trust God, he will show us how to change and grow into the people he wants us to be. Conversion happens again and again. It leads us to live our lives according to God's great love for us. God the Holy Spirit gives us this desire to change and grow.

Faith Word

conversion see p. 257

When have I experienced God's forgiveness?

Activity

Write a case study of a modern-day prodigal son or daughter. What did the person do to turn from God? What did the person's parent do when the son or daughter returned? Be sure to include a conclusion that shows that both God and the parent forgave the person. Now share your case study with a partner. What aspects of your case studies are alike? What aspects are different?

Grace makes us part of the life of the Trinity.

When we turn away from sin and back to God, we experience the work of God's love within us. This is God's grace, which is God's life that he shares with us. It is the free and undeserved help that God gives us to respond to his call. It is our participation in the life of God.

God's love was revealed to us in Jesus Christ and given to us by the Holy Spirit. Through our Baptism, we are born to new life. Through the power of the Holy Spirit, we take part in Christ's Passion and Resurrection. We become members of the Body of Christ, the Church.

By Baptism, grace makes us part of the life of the Trinity. We become adopted children of God, sharers in the life of Jesus Christ, and members of God's family.

Did You Know?

 Small changes can add up.

One Church, Many Cultures

Through Baptism, we become children of God. As members of God's family, we are called to care for his gifts and for each other. Water is one of the most important of God's gifts. In many cultures, it symbolizes new life and growth. Access to clean water is a human right that the Church promotes and works for around the world. Organizations such as Catholic Relief Services work with local populations to build wells and improve their water systems. They help people receive the clean water they need, especially for drinking. In this way, the Church works to care for all God's people wherever they live.

Activity

God's love is the greatest gift we can receive. Compose a short poem or song to express how you feel about being a child of God.

_____

_____

_____

_____

_____

_____

_____

Share your composition with a friend.

The Holy Spirit fills our hearts with sanctifying grace.

What do you normally do when you receive a gift? You open it! Most of us do not tuck gifts away on a closet shelf, wrapped, and forget about them. We remove the wrapping, thank the giver, and usually appreciate and use the gifts.

A powerful, life-giving gift that a person can receive does not come wrapped and tied with a bow. In fact, it is invisible to the eye. This gift is God's grace. Grace is the help God gives us to know and love God as his adopted children. Grace is invisible, but it is essential to a life of holiness. The grace God gives us helps us to be holy.

Faith Word

sanctifying grace
see p. 259

God freely offers us **sanctifying grace**, the gift of his life. It is infused into our soul to heal us of sin and make us holy. We receive sanctifying grace in Baptism. The other sacraments support and build upon this primary sacrament. It is God's divine life within us that makes us his children. Grace helps us to trust and believe in God. It strengthens us to live as Jesus did. We lose God's gift of sanctifying grace if we commit mortal sin. Grace is restored in the Sacrament of Penance.

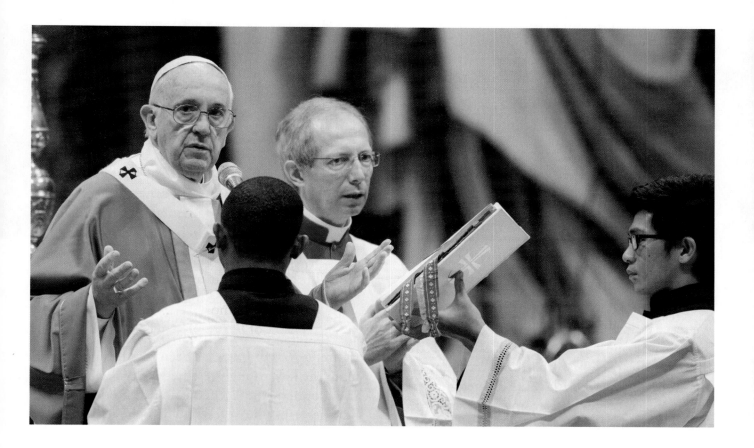

The Holy Spirit fills our souls with this grace, healing our souls and making them holy. Sanctifying grace enables us to live with God. It allows us to know and love God.

Reflect on what Pope Francis says about grace:

"We ought never to lose hope. God overwhelms us with his grace, if we keep asking."

"And with the grace of Baptism and of Eucharistic Communion I can become an instrument of God's mercy, of that beautiful mercy of God."

"The Eucharist is essential for us: it is Christ who wishes to enter our lives and fill us with his grace."

What Makes Us Catholic?

In the sacraments, we receive sanctifying grace, the gift of God's own life and friendship. To help us stay on the right path, we can ask for God's help. Through *actual grace*, God gives us the support we need along the way. Actual grace helps us avoid making wrong choices and can also help us to do good. The *Catechism of the Catholic Church* tells us that *"God has freely chosen to associate man with the work of his grace"* (CCC, 2008). God's grace works in us and brings us closer to our Father.

Faith Word

justification   see p. 257

Through Baptism and faith in Jesus Christ, we receive the gift of justification.

We receive another amazing gift through our Baptism and our faith in Jesus Christ. This is the gift of justification. **Justification** by faith means that through Jesus' Death and Resurrection, and the grace that comes to us from it, our sins are forgiven. We are also put into a right relationship with God. Justification moves us toward deeper conversion to God and helps us to cooperate with his grace. We are justified—freed from our sins and reconciled to God—through the power of the Holy Spirit. We become friends of God.

There is nothing we can do on our own to claim or deserve justification. Justification is an action of God. Through Baptism and faith in Jesus Christ, God's mercy and grace make it possible for us to be cleansed of our sins, reconciled to God, and sharers in eternal life with God. "The righteousness of God has been manifested apart from the law, though testified to by the law and the prophets, the righteousness of God through faith in Jesus Christ for all who believe. . . . All have sinned and are deprived of the glory of God. They are justified freely by his grace through the redemption in Christ Jesus, whom God set forth . . . to prove his righteousness in the present time, that he might be righteous and justify the one who has faith in Jesus" (Romans 3:21–26).

Partners in Faith

Saint Anselm

Saint Anselm was the archbishop of Canterbury. He is famous for teaching that faith and reason had to go together. He said that through reason, we are able to strengthen our faith, and through faith, we believe even what we cannot understand.

 Learn more about the life of Saint Anselm.

Faith Words

| conversion | sanctifying grace | justification |

 Show What You Know

Circle the correct answer to complete the sentences.

1. _____ is the action of God by which we receive his grace, are freed from sin, and are reconciled to God.

   a. Justification

   b. Sanctification

   c. Confirmation

2. A turning to God with all one's heart is called _____.

   a. complication

   b. contrition

   c. conversion

3. _____ is the gift of God's life that we receive in the sacraments.

   a. Sacramental grace

   b. Sanctifying grace

   c. Actual grace

Live Your Faith

• How do you experience justification in your life?

_____

_____

_____

_____

• The Holy Spirit gives us the desire to change and grow. How have you grown in your faith this year?

_____

_____

_____

_____

Mini-Task

The Parable of the Prodigal Son has a lot to teach us about God's love and forgiveness. The father represents God in the parable. He welcomes his lost son back with open arms. What about the brother in this story?

Read the Parable of the Prodigal Son in the Gospel of Luke 15:11–32. While you are reading, imagine yourself as the brother who stays with his father.

Why are you angry? Can you find it in your heart to forgive your lost sibling? In the space below, express your feelings in a letter to your sibling.

_____

_____

_____

_____

_____

_____

_____

_____

_____

_____

 Want to do more? Go to your Portfolio to continue this activity.

 At Home

As a family, talk about ways you can answer God's call to conversion. Make a list of ways your family can change and grow in God's love. With God's divine life in us through the gift of sanctifying grace, compose a family prayer answering God's call. Place the prayer on everyone's phone as a reminder to pray.

How do we become what we believe?

The Road to Emmaus

Unit Prayer

Leader: Saint Ignatius of Loyola wanted us to go forth and set the world on fire with our faith. In order to be a disciple of Christ, we must become what we believe. Spreading the faith that is in our hearts is how we can set the world on fire. Celebrating with our parish community at Mass helps us to become better followers of Jesus—to be his disciples.

Listen to the stories of missionary disciples among us helping to "set the world on fire."

Leader: Let us pray, starting with the Sign of the Cross.

In the name of the Father,
and of the Son,
and of the Holy Spirit. Amen.

O Lord, we gather at Mass with all your disciples to learn about your love and to praise your name. Help us to go forth and set the world on fire.

All: Go forth and set the world on fire.

Leader: O Lord, you feed us with your Word in the Scriptures at Mass. Teach us to go forth and set the world on fire.

All: Go forth and set the world on fire.

Leader: Lord Jesus, you feed us with your Body and your Blood in Holy Communion. Feed us to go forth and set the world on fire.

All: Go forth and set the world on fire.

End the Unit Prayer by singing the song for this unit.

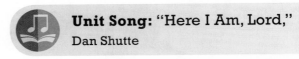

Unit Song: "Here I Am, Lord," Dan Shutte

Missionary Discipleship

When have you acted as Jesus wants? What did you do? Was it easy or hard? Has someone reached out to you when you felt alone or when it was hard to do as Jesus asks of you?

What is prayer?

When we pray, we raise our hearts and minds to God. We encounter God in prayer, especially in the sacraments. Prayer is a mystery in which we speak and listen to God. We address our prayers to God the Father, in Christ's name.

Go to the digital portal for a *Lectio* and *Visio Divina* prayer.

Prayer surges from the heart. It is a look toward heaven. It is a cry of love that embraces both suffering and joy.

Based on the words of Saint Thérèse of Lisieux

Prayer is raising our hearts and minds to God.

What are the keys to developing a good friendship with someone? You might name things such as: talking to the person, getting to know him, listening to her, making time for each other. These elements serve to build a strong relationship.

Prayer is a two-way relationship between God and us. When we pray, we raise our hearts and minds to God. Prayer includes many of the same characteristics of good friendships: talking, listening, making time, and sometimes just being quiet together. The first prayers we pray are those taught to us by others, usually in our families. These are prayers our parents pray for and with us, such as the Our Father, the Hail Mary, the Glory Be, nighttime prayers, or blessings before meals.

Faith Word

prayer see p. 258

We memorize these first prayers, but as we grow, prayer becomes something much deeper than simply reciting from memory. We begin to use our own words to express to God the longings of our minds and hearts. We also listen. We tune in to God's continual, abiding presence with us.

Something amazing happens when we realize that God is present in our lives. Over time we begin to recognize God's mysterious movement in our lives. Our friendship with God deepens. We hear his gentle words of love.

What was my first memory of prayer? What does prayer mean to me now?

Did You Know?

Prayer builds relationships.

Prayer brings God's people closer to him.

Why do we pray? Remember that God's desire is for us to know him and to love him. It is for this purpose that God created us.

"He made from one the whole human race to dwell on the entire surface of the earth, and he fixed the ordered seasons and the boundaries of their regions, so that people might seek God, . . . though indeed he is not far from any one of us" (Acts of the Apostles 17:26–27).

The deepest desire in our hearts is to seek and know God. This is why we pray. Prayer brings us closer to God.

Prayer is first and foremost the action of God. God tirelessly calls each of us into a relationship with him and his people, with Jesus Christ, and with the Holy Spirit. Our first step in prayer is to respond to God's invitation.

Both personal prayer and **communal prayer**— prayer we pray together as a community—help us to become aware of and remember God's presence. Some of our most meaningful experiences of prayer are within the community of the Church.

Communal prayer has been a part of the Church since her very beginning. The first disciples encountered God in their communal prayer life and especially in the breaking of the bread, or Eucharist.

Faith Word

communal prayer
see p. 257

One Church, Many Cultures

Communal prayer is an important part of the Catholic Church in Uganda. The Bukalongo shrine welcomes thousands of people from all religions for special New Year's Eve prayers and celebrations. The shrine also participates in *Essangalo*, its overnight communal prayer, held once a month, rain or shine. Prayer begins late in the evening, continues all night, and ends with a dawn Mass. *Essangalo* means "happiness" in several Ugandan dialects, and Church members call it a "happy vigil."

After Jesus' Resurrection, two of his disciples were walking to Emmaus, a village not far from Jerusalem. They were sad about Jesus' Death and had heard about the empty tomb. As they were talking, a stranger joined them. The disciples did not recognize him as the Risen Jesus. They told the stranger about the Death of Jesus and the empty tomb.

As they walked, Jesus taught them about Scripture. The disciples invited Jesus to have dinner with them. At this meal, Jesus took bread and blessed it. He then broke the bread and gave it to them.

The disciples then recognized Jesus. Imagine how close to him they must have felt in that moment of profound prayer! They returned to Jerusalem to tell others how Jesus "was made known to them in the breaking of the bread" (Luke 24:35).

Prayer and celebration of the Eucharist continued to bring God's people closer to him.

> "They devoted themselves to the teaching of the apostles and to the communal life, to the breaking of the bread and to the prayers. . . . Every day they devoted themselves to meeting together . . . and to breaking bread in their homes. . . . And every day the Lord added to their number those who were being saved."
>
> Acts of the Apostles 2:42, 46, 47

We, too, encounter God in prayer when we celebrate the sacraments. We pray with the Church when we celebrate the Sacrament of the Eucharist at Mass. We join a community of believers and together raise our hearts and minds to God through God's Word, through songs of praise and prayers of petition, and in thanksgiving for Jesus' gift of himself to us in Holy Communion.

What Makes Us Catholic?

Prayer leads us to Jesus, our light and our hope. The Apostles at the Last Supper experienced this when Jesus instituted the Eucharist. Jesus prayed and broke bread with the disciples in Emmaus, too. The words Jesus prayed brought the gift of Jesus himself to us. Pope Benedict XVI called our participation in the Eucharist "the highest point in all our prayer." When we receive the Eucharist, we "experience in an extraordinary manner the prayer that Jesus prayed, . . . that the transforming power of Christ's death and Resurrection may act within us." And Jesus continues to pray for us in the Eucharist. This is a prayer of love.

Activity

Review the story of the disciples on the road to Emmaus. With two friends, create a short skit that retells the story in your own words. Have one person play Jesus and the other two play the disciples. If there is time, switch roles so that each person gets to portray Jesus.

Prayer is a mystery in which we speak and listen to God.

There is hardly a page in the Gospels that in some way doesn't reveal Jesus as a man of prayer—speaking and listening to God, his Father. Jesus is a model for how we can speak and listen to God.

Jesus taught us to pray with patience and complete trust in God. He prayed in many ways. He thanked God the Father for his blessings and asked God to be with him. He prayed for the needs of others and forgave sinners in the name of his Father.

One of the most beautiful examples of the mystery and power of prayer in the Gospels is the Transfiguration of Jesus. We read that Jesus takes Peter, John, and James up the mountain to pray. In Luke's Gospel, the mountain is a regular place of prayer (see also Luke 6:12 and 22:39–41). In this prayerful encounter, Jesus gives his Apostles a glimpse of his divine glory. The Church celebrates this event every year on the Feast of the Transfiguration.

Mount Tabor in Israel is considered by Christians as the site of the Transfiguration of Jesus. The Church of the Transfiguration is at the top of the mountain.

"[Jesus] took Peter, John, and James and went up the mountain to pray. While he was praying his face changed in appearance and his clothing became dazzling white. And behold, two men were conversing with him, Moses and Elijah. . . . Peter and his companions had been overcome by sleep, but becoming fully awake, they saw his glory and the two men standing with him . . . . Then from the cloud came a voice that said, 'This is my chosen Son; listen to him.' After the voice had spoken, Jesus was found alone. They fell silent and did not at that time tell anyone what they had seen."

Luke 9:28–36

Activity

Look for the following words as you read the story of the Transfiguration. When you have checked off all the words, write down the word that stood out to you. Explain to the group why that word means something to you.

mountain	☐	cloud	☐
white	☐	Son	☐
sleep	☐	listen	☐
awake	☐	voice	☐
glory	☐	silent	☐

Prompted by the Holy Spirit, we address our prayers to God the Father in Christ's name.

Listen carefully the next time you are at Mass. Listen to the prayers the priest prays as well as your responses. You will notice something similar among them. You will recognize that they all follow a familiar pattern. First, they address God our Father. Because Jesus taught us to call God our Father, our prayers are primarily addressed to the Father, through the Son, and in the unity of the Holy Spirit. Next, they petition God for a particular need or a blessing. Sometimes they refer to a specific person, such as a saint or the Blessed Mother, and the prayer asks that we might have the courage to follow that person's example.

For instance, this is a prayer you would hear at Mass on the Feast of Saint Francis of Assisi:

"O God, by whose gift Saint Francis
was conformed to Christ in poverty
   and humility,
grant that, by walking in Francis' footsteps,
we may follow your Son,
and, through joyful charity,
come to be united with you.

Through our Lord Jesus Christ, your Son,
who lives and reigns with you in the unity of
   the Holy Spirit,
one God, for ever and ever."

Roman Missal, Feast of Saint Francis

Notice that this prayer begins "O God, . . ." and that it ends "Through our Lord Jesus Christ, your Son . . ." The prayers of the Church, when she celebrates the sacraments and the liturgy, are always addressed first to God the Father.

And as you can see from the prayer's ending, we pray to God the Father through—or in the name of—Jesus. Jesus, as truly human as we are human, is the way by which the Holy Spirit teaches us to pray to God the Father. Jesus is our connection point to God in prayer.

How we address our prayers to God in the Mass

"Almighty ever-living God . . . Through our Lord Jesus Christ, your Son . . ."

"O God . . . Through our Lord Jesus Christ, your Son . . ."

"Grant, we pray, almighty God . . . Through our Lord Jesus Christ, your Son . . ."

"Grant, O merciful God . . . Through Christ our Lord . . ."

"O God, you have taught us. . . . Through our Lord Jesus Christ, your Son . . ."

Partners in Faith

Thomas à Kempis

Thomas à Kempis' book *Imitation of Christ* is still popular five hundred years after it was written. Saint Thomas More said it was one book every Christian should read. Thomas à Kempis wrote a great deal about prayer and devotion. He also copied the Bible by hand four times! He served as a priest in the Netherlands. His favorite things to do were read, write, and pray.

 Learn more about the life of Thomas à Kempis.

Faith Words

prayer   **communal prayer**

 Show What You Know

Complete the sentences.

1. _____ taught us to pray with patience and complete trust in God.

2. _____ is raising our minds and hearts to God.

3. When we pray as a community, we participate in _____ prayer.

4. Our first step in prayer is to respond to God's _____.

Live Your Faith

• How would you explain to someone who has never prayed before how to raise your heart or your mind to God?

_____

_____

_____

_____

_____

_____

_____

• What form of communal prayer do you enjoy? Whom would you like to invite to join you in communal prayer?

_____

_____

_____

_____

_____

_____

How is prayer strengthening my relationship with God and others?

Mini-Task

In today's digital world, apps can help us keep track of daily responsibilities such as homework. They also give us information, entertain us through games and videos, and connect us to our friends and family.

In the space below, design and title your own prayer app. What would it do? How would it help connect you with God and your friends?

My Prayer App: _____

 Want to do more? Go to your Portfolio to continue this activity.

At Home

In prayer, we deepen our friendship with God. Talk with your family members about their friendship with God. How do all of them feel that God is their friend? As a family, take time this week to speak and listen to God as your friend.

Why do we pray?

Prayer is an essential part of our Sacred Tradition. The Holy Spirit teaches the Church and her members to pray. We pray together in the liturgy and the sacraments. Prayer builds our trust in God. Prayer is at the heart of the Christian life.

Go to the digital portal for a prayer of thanksgiving.

"Our prayer cannot be reduced to an hour on Sundays. It is important to have a daily relationship with the Lord."

Pope Francis

Prayer is an essential part of Sacred Tradition.

One of the ways that we learn new things is with the help of a good teacher. But we have to want to learn. One of the most important things we will ever learn how to do is to pray. It is not enough to know what Sacred Scripture tells us about prayer. We have to learn *how* to pray. And for this, we look to the Sacred Tradition of the Church. There, our teacher, the Holy Spirit, teaches the Church to pray as a community.

The Holy Spirit is the living water within us that points us to Christ. Like drawing water to drink from a well, we can draw from the well of God's Word as a source for our prayer. We also draw from the well of the Church's sacraments as a source for our prayer. In the liturgy, Christ and the Holy Spirit are at work proclaiming, making present, and communicating the mystery of salvation. As people of faith, we bring prayerful hearts to the Church's celebration of the sacraments to seek the Lord and to hear and keep his Word.

Over the centuries, many holy men and women have studied and reflected deeply on what prayer is and how to pray. They have shared with us the wealth of their knowledge and experience as people of prayer. They are a part of the Sacred Tradition of the Church through whom the Holy Spirit teaches us to pray.

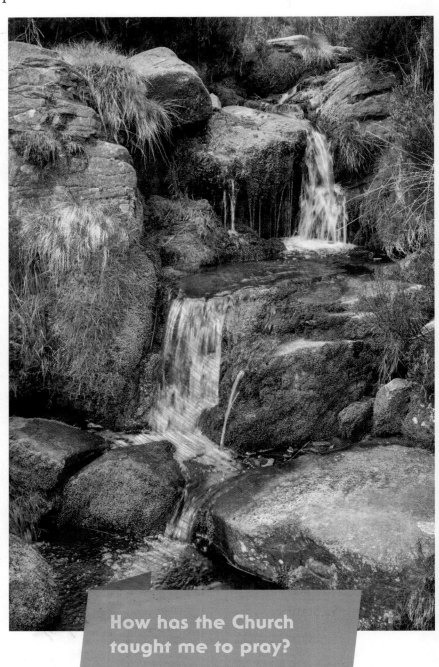

How has the Church taught me to pray?

Did You Know?

God's Word is a source of prayer.

Prayer builds our trust in God.

How do we get to the point where we can trust in the Lord with all our hearts, totally rely on him, and be mindful of him always?

In the Lord's Prayer, we pray to God the Father with the trust of children who look to their Father for everything that is good and beautiful. God the Father gives us everything that we need: "Give us this day our daily bread."

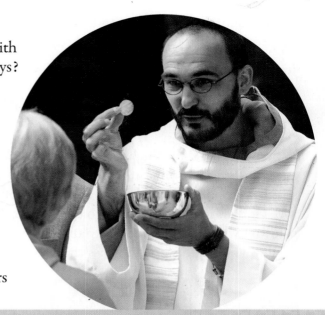

Notice that Jesus did not tell us to pray "Give me this day my daily bread." When we pray the Our Father, we are participating in the fulfillment of God's covenant promises to his people. When we gather as Church and pray "Give us this day, . . ." as we do in the Church's liturgy and sacraments, we pray to God, the Father of *all*, for the needs of our brothers and sisters.

Our trust in God grows through our prayerful participation in the liturgy and sacraments of the Church. God responds to our prayer, most especially in the Eucharist, where we receive the nourishment of our "daily bread."

> "Trust in the LORD with all your heart,
> on your own intelligence do not rely;
> In all your ways be mindful of him,
> and he will make straight your paths."
>
> Proverbs 3:5–6

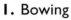

Activity

Did you know that you can pray not only with your words, but also with your body? Saint Dominic said there are nine ways to pray with your body:

1. Bowing

2. Lying facedown on the floor

3. Repeating "Have mercy on me, O God" while sitting or standing

4. Genuflecting

5. Standing with open hands before a crucifix

6. Standing with arms outstretched

7. Standing with arms raised above the head

8. Sitting and reading Scripture

9. Walking in silence

Place a check mark next to any of these ways that you have *never* prayed before. Take a few minutes to pray in one of these ways.

In the Eucharist, the source and summit of the Church's life and prayer, God gives us the Bread of Life.

Jesus said: "I am the bread of life. . . . I am the living bread that came down from heaven; whoever eats this bread will live forever; and the bread that I will give is my flesh for the life of the world" (John 6:48, 51).

When we receive the Eucharist in Holy Communion, we receive the wondrous gift of God's grace in us. With this grace and the spiritual food that is the Body and Blood of Christ, we can love God and open our hearts to the needs of those around us, to those who hunger physically and spiritually. Our trust in God—who desires nothing less than to live in us—grows.

One Church, Many Cultures

Each culture has distinct customs and ways of living. Catholics living in non-Christian countries often follow certain local customs while also remaining true to their faith. For example, in some predominantly Muslim countries, Sunday is not considered a weekend day or the day of rest. Though they often cannot rest from work on Sundays, Catholics in these countries still make time to attend Mass and spend time with family. In countries where any public Christian practice or worship is forbidden, such as Saudi Arabia, Catholics and other Christians cannot attend Mass or church services. Often they pray at home as a family and seek other personal ways to keep Sunday holy.

Partners in Faith

Saint Louise de Marillac

Saint Louise de Marillac felt that God wanted her to be a nun, but she was already married. While she was praying, God told Louise that there would be a time when she would be a nun. After her husband's death, she did become a nun. She spent the rest of her life working with the poor.

 Learn more about the life of Saint Louise de Marillac.

The Church prays together in the liturgy and the sacraments.

Why do we pray? We do so because it is a necessity for us as Christians (see *CCC*, 2757). It is impossible to be a disciple, or live the Christian life, without prayer. Prayer and living as a Christian are inseparable. Saint Paul tells us: "Pray without ceasing. In all circumstances give thanks, for this is the will of God for you in Christ Jesus" (1 Thessalonians 5:17–18).

Saint Paul would be happy to know that over the centuries, the Church has taken his words to heart. At any moment on any day, somewhere in the world, the Church is at prayer in the liturgy and sacraments.

Communal prayer, or praying as the Church, is an important dimension of our lives as people who pray. As members of the Body of Christ, the Church, we join together to pray together in the liturgy and sacraments.

The communal prayer of the Church includes the **Liturgy of the Hours**. Bishops, priests, deacons, men and women religious, and laypeople come together to pray the Liturgy of the Hours in the morning and evening, and at other times of the day. The Liturgy of the Hours includes songs and psalms, Scripture readings, the Lord's Prayer, and other readings and responses. The Church has prayed the Liturgy of the Hours for centuries. While it is a communal prayer, it can also be prayed alone.

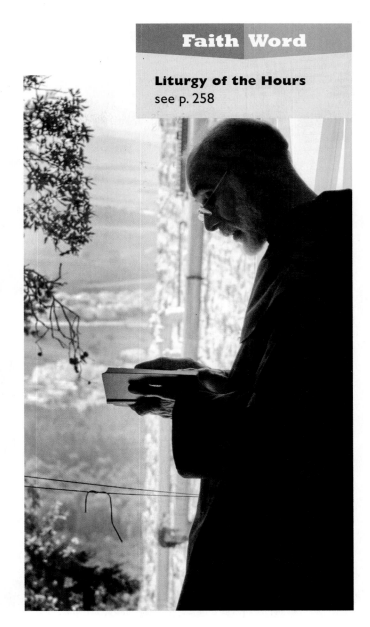

Faith Word

Liturgy of the Hours
see p. 258

What Makes Us Catholic?

The Liturgy of the Hours is the liturgical prayer of the Church. Early Christians gathered for prayer at certain times throughout the day. They recited the Psalms of the Old Testament and read from the New Testament. In later years, Church leaders and those in religious orders mainly prayed the Liturgy of the Hours. They used a special prayer book called the Breviary. Beginning in the 1970s, though, the bishops encouraged the whole Church to pray the Liturgy of the Hours. Even if we pray it alone, we know that others are praying, too. The Liturgy of the Hours is the prayer of the entire Church.

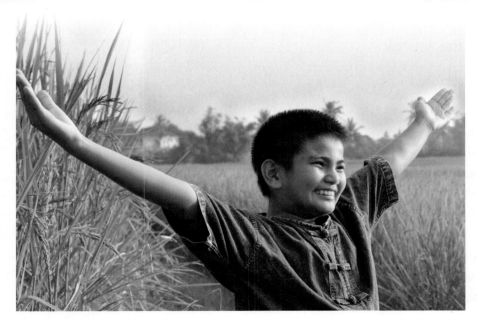

Prayer is at the heart of Christian life.

The *Catechism* tells us that "Prayer is the life of the new heart. It ought to animate us at every moment . . . ; prayer is a remembrance of God often awakened by the memory of the heart" (*CCC*, 2697). Saint Gregory of Nazianzus reminds us that we should remember God more often than we breathe!

Imagine a life of prayer so deep, so connected to God, that we remember God more often than we breathe. Prayer is at the heart of Christian life. Like breath, which is life, the heart is life. These are two profound images about the place of prayer in our lives.

Does this mean that we must be constantly falling to our knees in prayer? No, but what it does mean is that we remember God's presence in the world and in our lives at all times. This is the deep, meaningful kind of remembering where we consciously remember and acknowledge God's presence—in our history *and* right now. Then our lives do become a prayer offered to God. We become aware that God is present and connected to us as we move through and focus on the ordinary moments and tasks of our day. It's as if we say "Here I am, God. And I know you are here, too."

The most profound connection we have with God is in the Eucharistic liturgy, which is the fullest or most complete expression of the Church's communal prayer. At the celebration of the Eucharist we gather, listen to God's Word, and are nourished by the Real Presence of Jesus in the Eucharist. The Eucharist is the "source and summit" of the Church's life, because in it, Christ unites us with his sacrifice on the Cross.

Activity

Work with a partner or in small groups to discuss and answer the questions below. Write your answers in the space provided.

How is the Eucharist the source of our life?	How is the Eucharist the summit of our life?

Show What You Know

In your own words, write a definition for the term.

Liturgy of the Hours

_____

_____

Fill in the blanks to complete the sentences.

1. Prayer is at the center of our Christian _____ .

2. The _____ is the source and summit of the Church's life.

3. The _____ teaches the Church to pray as a community.

Live Your Faith

• What kinds of prayers do you like to pray alone? What kinds of prayer do you like to pray as part of communal prayer?

_____

_____

_____

_____

_____

_____

• How can you be mindful of God in prayer and in your everyday life?

_____

_____

_____

_____

_____

_____

What are the ways I pray?

Mini-Task

Sing and Pray Twice

There are many ways to pray. In the activity on page 155, we read some of the ways Saint Dominic said we can pray with our bodies.

Another way to pray is with song. Saint Augustine said that when we sing, we pray twice.

Write your own song that expresses an aspect of prayer. You can set the words to music that you write or to the melody of another song that you like.

How does your prayer-song inspire you? Write down your thoughts and share with the group.

_____

_____

_____

_____

_____

_____

_____

_____

Want to do more? Go to your Portfolio to continue this activity.

At Home

Have your family take a moment to remember God's presence during a time when you do not ordinarily pray. Quietly think or say: "Here we are, God. We are here. And we know that you are here, too." Ask family members to tell one way they know God is with them in prayer.

How do we pray?

Christians around the world pray in different ways, but everywhere around the world, people are praying with the Church all day long and all through the year. Our prayers bring us closer to God. The Church prays together in her liturgy. We can also pray using the five basic forms of prayer and with prayers spoken in the silence of our hearts.

Go to the digital portal for a prayer of blessing.

"This is a prayer we must pray every day: 'Holy Spirit, make my heart open to the Word of God, make my heart open to goodness, make my heart open to the beauty of God every day.'"

Pope Francis

Christians around the world gather in communal prayer.

Jesus said: "Where two or three are gathered in my name, there I am in the midst of them" (Matthew 18:20). Whenever we gather to pray with our family, friends, or parish, we raise our voices together as one. We join our voices with the voice of the whole Church, united with Christ.

We are called to be a community of faith. When we pray together, we proclaim what we believe together. Take a moment to think about this fact: All around the world right now, Christians are at prayer. At any given moment in any given place, the Holy Spirit is at work in the Church, helping us remember all that Jesus taught us. The Holy Spirit never stops teaching us how to pray.

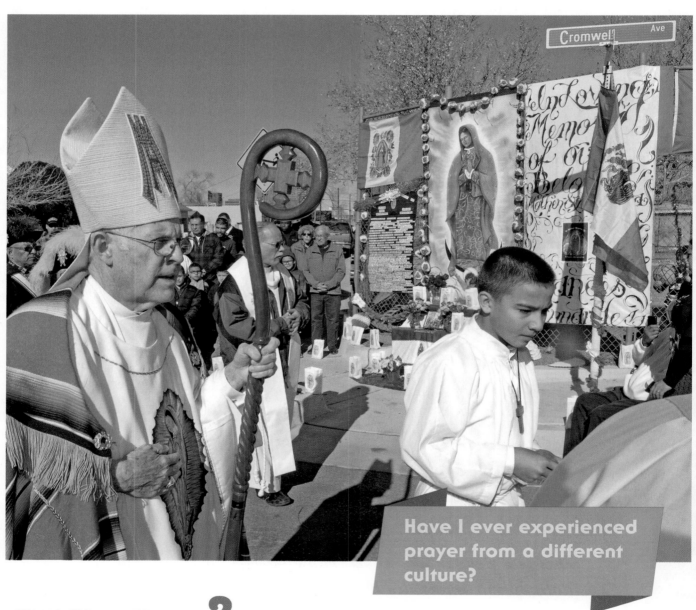

Have I ever experienced prayer from a different culture?

Did You Know?

We can pray with music from our own culture.

Faith Word

intention see p. 257

Our regular prayers bring us closer to God.

Have you ever sat at your desk at school and taken an extremely difficult test? Maybe you muttered the words (in your head because there's no talking during tests): "O God, help me!" Even in this short prayer, your **intention** is what brings you closer to God.

The Church invites us to pray all the time. The Holy Spirit also guides our personal prayer. With the help of the Holy Spirit, we pray these basic forms of prayer: blessing, petition, intercession, thanksgiving, and praise. To bless is to dedicate someone or something to God or to make something holy in God's name. God continually blesses us with many gifts. Because God first blessed us, we, too, can pray for his blessing on people and things.

Prayers of petition are prayers in which we ask something of God. Asking for forgiveness is the most important type of petition. Intercession is a type of petition in which we ask for something on behalf of another person or a group of people.

Prayers of thanksgiving show our gratitude to God for all he has given us. We show our gratitude most especially for the life, Passion, Death, and Resurrection of Jesus. We do this when we pray the greatest prayer of the Church, the Eucharist.

Prayers of praise give glory to God for being God. Prayers of praise do not involve our needs or our gratitude. We praise God simply because he is God.

The Church prays together in the liturgy.

One of the wonderful things that happens at Baptism is that we become members of a community whose purpose is to love and serve God. This community is the Church. The Holy Spirit has, from the Church's beginning, provided her with everything necessary to love and serve God in the best way possible. One of these ways is through prayer.

The Church unites all of God's people in prayer. She invites us to pray on our own or with others, every day. In the liturgy, the Church participates in the work of God. Through her sacramental celebrations, the Church participates in the saving work of Christ. We can join with the Church in praying the Liturgy of the Hours, in participating at Mass, and in celebrating all the feasts commemorating the Blessed Mother and all the saints throughout the year.

When we are at Mass, we join together as the Body of Christ in prayers of forgiveness, petition, praise, and thanksgiving to God. We prayerfully listen and respond during the Liturgy of the Word and the Liturgy of the Eucharist.

Activity

Here is a partial list of prayer responses that we pray together as the assembly during Mass on Sunday. How many more can you add?

Responses:

"And with your Spirit."

"Amen."

After first and second Scripture readings: "Thanks be to God."

After the Gospel: "Praise to you, Lord Jesus Christ."

Prayer of the Faithful: "Lord, hear our prayer."

What Makes Us Catholic?

The Liturgy of the Hours always includes praying psalms. These are beautiful and ancient prayers from the Bible. When we say or sing the psalms, we are following Jesus' example of prayer. For the Liturgy of the Hours, the source of the psalms is from a book called the **Psalter**. The Psalter arranges the psalms in a special order according to the time of day and the liturgical season. The psalms help us to praise **God** through the many seasons of the Catholic Church.

Certain prayers are spoken in the silence of our hearts.

In the Christian tradition, there are three major forms of prayer: vocal prayer, **meditation**, and **contemplation**. Meditation and contemplation are forms of silent prayer. This is prayer spoken in the silence of our hearts.

Meditation is a quest to understand the why and how of being a disciple of Christ (see *CCC*, 2705). Meditation uses our thoughts, imagination, and emotions to focus on God and what he wants us to know. We can meditate on what we read, especially Sacred Scripture, on what we hear, or on what our senses experience in God's creation. Meditation is prayerful reflection guided by the Holy Spirit, which takes us into the heart of Jesus.

Contemplation is being with Jesus. Saint Teresa of Ávila described it as a conversation with a close friend. In contemplative prayer, our mind is quieter, or less active, than when we meditate. We simply sit in the presence of God and listen for his voice. All of our attention is fixed on God.

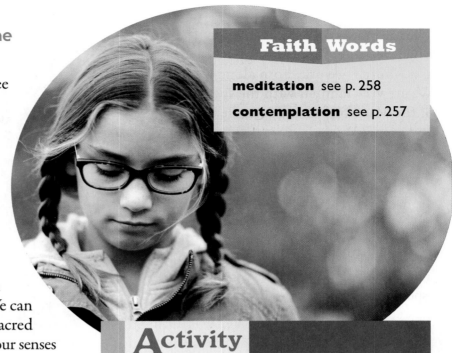

Faith Words

meditation see p. 258

contemplation see p. 257

Activity

You can learn how to meditate or contemplate through practice. Start by sitting in a comfortable position. Fold your hands on your lap in prayer. Close your eyes. Now imagine that Jesus is in front of you. Imagine what he is saying to you. For a few minutes, think about what he is telling you. Then open your eyes and write down what came to mind.

Partners in Faith

Saint Andrew Kim Taegŏn

The Korean martyrs are 124 Christians who were killed for their faith in the nineteenth century. Christianity was not allowed in Korea at the time, and Christians had to practice in secret. Saint Andrew Kim Taegŏn, the patron saint of Korea, was the first Korean-born Catholic priest. His parents were converts, and he was raised a Catholic. His father was also killed for being a Christian.

 Learn more about the life of Saint Andrew Kim Taegŏn.

The celebration of Mass is an example of how, when we gather for the liturgy and pray together as a Church, we pray both aloud and silently. We are very familiar with the spoken prayers of the Mass, but what about the times of quiet and silence?

One such moment of silence happens when we first enter the church. We kneel and pray before Mass to prepare ourselves to celebrate the Eucharist. Another time of silence occurs after we listen to God's Word in the Liturgy of the Word. First we respond vocally: "Praise to you, Lord Jesus Christ." Then we meditate on what we have heard, especially in the quiet moments after the homily.

The most profound time of silence is during the Liturgy of the Eucharist, when we receive Jesus in Holy Communion. Jesus becomes a part of us. We kneel in silence, just being with Jesus. This is a prayer of contemplation. In this moment of prayer, breathed in the silence of our hearts, we are as close to Jesus as we can be.

One Church, Many Cultures

Catholics brought Christianity to Korea more than two hundred years ago. In recent years, the Catholic Church in South Korea has grown rapidly. While relatively small compared with the total population, the number of Catholics has nearly doubled in the past ten years. And more and more Korean young people are considering the priesthood and religious vocations. Pope Francis visited South Korea in 2014. He celebrated Mass at Myeongdong Cathedral in Seoul and honored Korean martyrs. Catholics gathered to join their prayers to those of the martyrs.

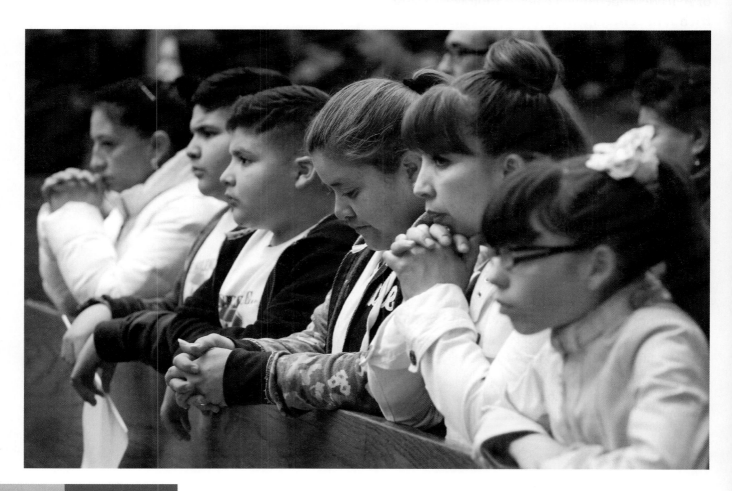

Faith Words

**intention   meditation
contemplation**

 ## Show What You Know

Match the terms to the correct definitions.

1. contemplation

prayer that uses our thoughts, imagination, and emotions to focus on God and what he wants us to know

2. intention

wordless, silent prayer in which we focus entirely on God and our being in his presence

3. meditation

the aim of our prayers or plan for them

Live Your Faith

• Which kind of prayer is easier for you to pray, meditation or contemplation? Why?

_____

_____

_____

_____

• Choose one of the five basic forms of prayer and write your own prayer in that form.

_____

_____

_____

_____

• What is your prayer intention this week?

_____

_____

_____

_____

How do I integrate prayer into daily life?

Mini-Task

There are many types of prayer. Praying with Scripture in a reflective manner is called *Lectio Divina*. We also pray while meditating on sacred art through *Visio Divina*, and reflecting upon and meditating to music is called *Audio Divina*. On the lines below, write the song title and lyrics of a song you know that inspires you to reflect on God's love.

_____

_____

_____

_____

_____

_____

_____

_____

_____

_____

_____

_____

Share the information about your song with a partner. If you can, listen to the song that inspires your partner.

Want to do more? Go to your Portfolio to continue this activity.

At Home

Your family is praying with your Church family all over the world. Have each of your family members voice an intention for the whole family. Pray on these intentions together silently for a few minutes.

What helps us to pray?

When we gather to pray with the Church at Eucharist, we are united as a family in Christ with all believers. We are united with the Communion of Saints with whom we join to offer prayer and praise. The family is our first community of prayer. Our faith helps us pray when it is hard to do so.

Go to the digital portal for a prayer of praise.

"It is truly right and just, our duty and our salvation,
always and everywhere to give you thanks, Father most holy,
through your beloved Son, Jesus Christ, your Word through whom you made all things."

Roman Missal, Eucharistic Prayer II

The Communion of Saints is united at prayer in the Eucharist.

"I believe in . . . the Communion of Saints . . . "
(The Apostles' Creed).

We profess our belief in the **Communion of Saints** every time we recite the Apostles' Creed at Mass. The English word *saint* can translate in Latin into two words: *sancti* ("holy people") and *sancta* ("holy things"). Knowing these meanings helps us realize that this is what the Church is: the communion of holy people and holy things.

The Church is a communion of holy, faithful people who are living and those who have died but are alive with God in heaven or Purgatory. The Church is also a communion of holy things. These holy things refer to the sacraments, particularly the Eucharist.

To profess that we are a part of the Communion of Saints is to say two things: we are connected

Faith Word

Communion of Saints
see p. 257

to all faithful people living now and those who have died, and we are united as the one Body of Christ through "holy things," especially the Eucharist.

When we celebrate the Eucharist, the Church asks God's mercy for the entire Communion of Saints— all believers, those living on earth and those who have died. The next time you are at Mass, remember that the entire Communion of Saints is there, praising and thanking God with you!

This community of heaven and earth is expressed beautifully in the Litany of the Saints. It is often prayed during the most solemn feasts of the liturgical year.

How does it feel knowing I am connected to the Communion of Saints?

Did You Know?

The Eucharist feeds the Church.

The Church's liturgy offers prayer and praise.

When we want water to drink, bathe, or wash our clothes, we turn on the faucet. We probably do not think a lot about the source of the water that flows out of the tap. Millions of people around the world draw their water from wells. When a well runs dry, the people's physical well-being is threatened, because water is necessary for life.

The *Catechism of the Catholic Church* tells us that "the Holy Spirit is the *living water* 'welling up to eternal life' in the heart that prays" (*CCC*, 2652). Christ is the source of this living water. As Jesus told the woman at the well, this living water is necessary for eternal life.

> "Everyone who drinks this water will be thirsty again; but whoever drinks the water I shall give will never thirst; the water I shall give will become in him a spring of water welling up to eternal life."
> John 4:13–14

One of the Church's spiritual wells that enables us to drink of the Holy Spirit is the liturgy. When the Church gathers to celebrate liturgy, "the mission of Christ and of the Holy Spirit proclaims, makes present, and communicates the mystery of salvation, which is continued in the heart that prays" (*CCC*, 2655). When we pray during the Church's liturgy, we pray with the Church. We make the Church's prayer a part of ourselves. Liturgy is the prayer of the Church, and it is always prayed in communion with the Blessed Trinity.

The Church's liturgy is a source of prayer from which we can draw the "living water" Jesus gives. We offer prayer and praise to God in the liturgy.

One Church, Many Cultures

It is important for a community to have access to clean, safe water. Catholic World Mission (CWM) works around the globe to share the Word of God and help people who live in poverty. In Ghana, CWM is working with local people to build water wells in the village schools, medical clinics, and other public buildings. Before the wells were built, people sometimes had to walk several miles every day to find clean water. Now the children and their families can focus on their schoolwork or jobs.

Activity

The Holy Spirit is the living water. We can draw this living water from the liturgy. Work with a partner to write what these statements mean. Use your explanation to teach another pair about the relationship between the Holy Spirit and the liturgy.

The family is our first school of prayer.

For most of us, the first place we meet Jesus is in our families. We do not often think of our families as a school, but in a real sense, our families are a school of prayer, our *first* school of prayer, because we first learn to pray in our families.

Our homes are meant to be places of prayer where we learn Christian virtues and how to love one another. Our homes are communities of grace where God is present. We pray together at home in many ways—grace before and after meals, blessings to greet the day and to end the day, special prayers for special events and occasions in our lives, and family prayers, rituals, and traditions throughout the Church's liturgical year, such as Advent, Christmas, Lent, and Easter.

We pray together with our families at church, too. It is with our families that we first learn to pray with the Church in her liturgies. The celebration of the Sacraments of Christian Initiation are big moments in the lives of Catholic families. We gather to celebrate Baptisms, First Holy Communion, and Confirmation. We attend Sunday Mass every week with our families. All of these are ways that the family prays together. These experiences of praying, both at home and with the Church community in her liturgies, contribute to what makes a family holy.

What Makes Us Catholic?

There are many ways Catholic families can participate in worldwide prayer. Every January, for example, the Church celebrates a World Day of Peace. With the pope, we pray that peace will reign in our hearts. Prayer events may have a specific theme, such as the World Day of Prayer for the Care of Creation started by Pope Francis. Other worldwide opportunities for prayer include World Day of the Poor and World Youth Day. Even if an event is held in a faraway place, we can still join in the prayer celebration. Your parish may hold a special service on these days. Or you may join your family in prayer at home.

Our faith supports our prayers.

As people of faith, one of the things that we can know with certainty is that God is always there when we pray, even when it does not seem that he is. It is not uncommon to struggle in one's prayer life. That struggle is also not something to worry about. One of the main difficulties we can have in the practice of prayer is distraction. So many things in life compete for our time and attention. At other times, our prayer seems dry and empty. It might seem as if God is not listening, or not even there.

Sometimes when we pray, we might feel alone, afraid, or full of doubt. We might feel bored or even tempted to stop praying altogether. Prayer might just seem ordinary. These experiences can happen when we pray alone, with others, and even during Mass. And in all of these challenging experiences, God is very much present with us.

Activity

Think about the ways we are distracted when we are trying to pray. Check off any of these ways that have distracted you. Then tell how you were able to put your focus back on God.

Distraction	Has this happened to you?	What did you do?
There's too much noise around me.		
I get interrupted.		
I feel bored.		
I do not know what to pray for or about.		
I feel ashamed or unready to talk to God.		

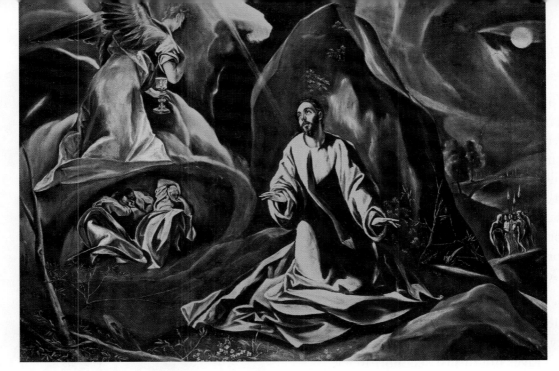

Agony in the Garden of Gethsemane by El Greco, 1590s

On the night before his Passion and Death, Jesus prayed in the Garden of Gethsemane (see John 17). His prayer to God the Father can teach us to persevere in prayer through the most difficult struggles in life. Tradition calls this prayer the "high priestly prayer" of Jesus. It is the longest prayer of Jesus we find in the Gospel. He knows that the next day he will face his Passion and Death. Yet Jesus didn't run away from the suffering and the Cross that awaited him. He did not run away from his Father's will. His was the prayer of pure faith. He persevered in prayer, knowing that it was the Father's will, not his, that needed to be accomplished.

With faith, nourished with the Bread of Life, we can persevere in prayer, too. At Mass, the memorial of Christ's Passover, Christ himself, the eternal High Priest, offers the Eucharistic sacrifice. Our participation in this Holy Sacrifice unites us to Christ and nourishes us with the strength we need to live faithfully.

Partners in Faith

Saints Felicity and Perpetua

Saints Felicity and Perpetua are among the saints named in Eucharistic Prayer I of the Mass. Perpetua was a Roman noblewoman and young mother. Felicity was a slave. They were Christians at a time in the Roman Empire when Christians were persecuted for their faith. Together, they were imprisoned and put to death for being Christians. We honor them for their faithfulness to God even in times of great challenge.

 Learn more about the lives of Saints Felicity and Perpetua.

Faith Word

Communion of Saints

 Show What You Know

In your own words, give a short explanation for each term. Compare your responses with a partner's.

Communion of Saints

_____

_____

_____

perseverance in prayer

_____

_____

_____

the liturgy as "living water"

_____

_____

_____

Live Your Faith

• How do the sacraments strengthen your prayer life?

_____

_____

_____

_____

_____

_____

• What could you say to someone who feels too distracted to pray?

_____

_____

_____

_____

_____

_____

Who helps me to pray?

Mini-Task

The Communion of Saints reminds us that we are always connected to our brothers and sisters in faith. The Litany of the Saints is a prayer for the intercession of the saints. It includes a list or "litany" of many canonized saints and martyrs.

In the space below, write your own Litany of the Saints. You can start with the names of people in the New Testament who were close to Jesus. You can also ask your siblings who have celebrated Confirmation, parents, and grandparents what their Confirmation name was. This name is usually the name of a saint!

My Litany of the Saints

All you holy men and women, pray for us.

Saint _____ and Saint _____

Pray for us.

Saint _____ and Saint _____

Pray for us.

Saint _____ and Saint _____

Pray for us.

Saint _____ and Saint _____

Pray for us.

All you holy men and women, pray for us!

Amen.

Want to do more? Go to your Portfolio to continue this activity.

At Home

Who are some saints that are important in your family's life? In your family prayers at night or at meals, ask those saints to pray for you. The next time your family is at Mass, remember that you are joined to the Communion of Saints in prayer.

Why is the Lord's Prayer called the perfect prayer?

The Lord's Prayer expresses the Church's hope in God. Through it, we are united with the Trinity. When we pray the Lord's Prayer, we glorify God and show our trust that he hears us.

Go to the digital portal for a meditation prayer.

"God thirsts for us so that we may thirst for him. Prayer is an encounter between God's thirst and our own."

Saint Augustine

The Lord's Prayer expresses the Church's hope in God.

Have you ever wondered why nearly every time the Church gathers to pray, we pray the Lord's Prayer? This is because the Lord's Prayer, or the Our Father, is the perfect prayer. It is the summary of the whole Gospel.

From the time of the first Christians, the Lord's Prayer has been the prayer of the Church. In fact, the first Christian communities prayed it three times a day. The Church has prayed it ever since, usually as a part of her liturgy. It is prayed in the Liturgy of the Hours and during the celebration of certain sacraments, most especially the Eucharist.

Have you ever wondered why we pray the Lord's Prayer at every Mass? Or why we pray it when we do during Mass? The Lord's Prayer is placed within the Liturgy of the Eucharist. We pray it after the Eucharistic Prayer and before Holy Communion. We pray it *after* the Eucharistic Prayer because it sums up all of our prayers of petition and intercession that we have just prayed. We pray it *before* Holy Communion because it is our prayer of expectation that the Lord will come again. We express our hope in the fulfillment of God's Kingdom.

When do I pray the Lord's Prayer?

Did You Know?

The first apostles prayed the Lord's Prayer.

The Lord's Prayer unites us with God the Father and with his Son, Jesus Christ.

There are many passages in the Gospels that reveal the relationship between God the Father and his divine Son, Jesus. Often these are Jesus' own words. For example:

"All things have been handed over to me by my Father. No one knows the Son except the Father, and no one knows the Father except the Son and anyone to whom the Son wishes to reveal him" (Matthew 11:27).

"I am the true vine, and my Father is the vine grower" (John 15:1).

"As the Father loves me, so I also love you. Remain in my love. If you keep my commandments, you will remain in my love, just as I have kept my Father's commandments and remain in his love" (John 15:9–10).

"Everything that the Father has is mine" (John 16:15).

One Church, Many Cultures

Scripture has references to vineyards, vines, grapes, and wine. Jesus even uses this imagery when he calls himself the "true vine." We are Jesus' disciples, the branches of the true vine. These images may also come to mind when we think of the Eucharist. The wine consecrated at Mass is made from grapes, a gift of the earth and the work of human hands. Some monastic communities keep vineyards. The monks pray, work the land, and make wine. We offer the gift of wine at every celebration of the Mass. Once consecrated, it becomes the gift of Jesus' Blood in the Eucharist.

Activity

There are two versions of the Lord's Prayer in the Gospels. Work in small groups to read Matthew 6:9–13 and Luke 11:2–4. Then answer the questions.

1. How are the two versions alike?

2. What are some of their differences?

Write your answers on the lines below. Which version is closest to the prayer you know by heart?

_____

_____

_____

_____

_____

_____

_____

_____

_____

_____

_____

The Solitude of Christ by **Maurice Denis, 1918**

When Jesus taught his disciples how to pray, saying "Our Father. . . ," he invited them into a new, close relationship with his heavenly Father. Through his Death and Resurrection, Jesus has made it possible for us to share in the life of God. He called us his brothers and sisters (see Matthew 12:48–50). He revealed God as his Father and as our Father. Through Christ, we are the adopted children of God:

"In love he destined us for adoption to himself through Jesus Christ, in accord with the favor of his will, for the praise of the glory of his grace that he granted us in the beloved " (Ephesians 1:4–6).

We pray "Our Father," not "Your Father" or "My Father." When we say *Our* Father, we proclaim the truth that through our Baptism, we are united to each other in communion with the Blessed Trinity. We express this unity in all of the celebrations of the sacraments, beginning with Baptism and Confirmation. The Lord's Prayer signifies new birth into the life of God. When we pray the Lord's Prayer, we are united with God and Jesus, his Son, the Holy Spirit, and with each other through our Baptism.

What Makes Us Catholic?

The word *father* is an important way to describe certain people in the Church. We call some early Church leaders and teachers our *Church Fathers*. Priests are called *Fathers* as well, for they guide and care for the people of their parish. The connection to family continues in the way some monks are called *Brothers* and some women religious are called *Sisters*. Regardless of the title, we all believe in and worship our one heavenly Father. Praying the Lord's Prayer, or the Our Father, is one of the best ways to remind ourselves that God is our loving Father.

We glorify God in the Lord's Prayer.

When the Church prays, she always addresses God the Father first. When Jesus teaches his disciples to pray, he makes it very clear that our prayer is all about God first. All glory and praise belongs to God, our Father. The Lord's Prayer focuses our minds and hearts on God first. When we pray the Lord's Prayer in the liturgy, in the celebration of the sacraments, and in our personal prayers and devotions, we glorify God.

The first three petitions of the Lord's Prayer glorify God. In the first petition, "hallowed be thy name," we glorify God's name. *Hallowed* means "holy." In the Lord's Prayer, we do more than just say that God's name is holy. We ask God to help us glorify him by glorifying his name. We pray for reverence and wonder at the awesomeness of God.

In the second petition, "thy kingdom come," we give glory to God, whose reign of peace, justice, and love has been fulfilled in the Death and Resurrection of Jesus. Jesus teaches us to pray for the coming of the **Kingdom of God** at the end of time. Our prayer also reminds us that we are a part of God's Kingdom here and now by God's grace and by how we live. At Mass, we experience the Kingdom of God in our midst in the Eucharist—Jesus himself is present. At the end of Mass, the priest or deacon sends us forth, saying: "Go in peace, glorifying the Lord by your life."

The third petition, "thy will be done," gives glory to God by reminding us that our lives aren't about

Faith Word

Kingdom of God see p. 257

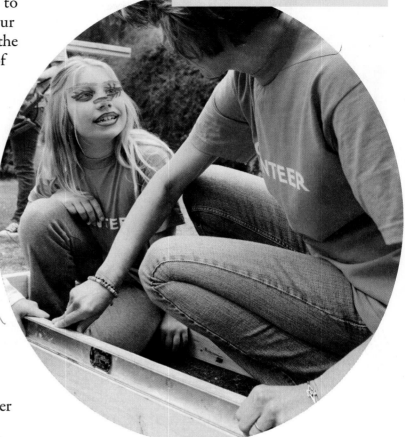

what we want but about what *God* wants. We unite our will with Jesus, who taught us to "love one another. As I have loved you, so you also should love one another" (John 13:34). To love and to be loved is to glorify God and to experience a taste of heaven. The Eucharist nourishes us to love with Jesus' love and to follow God's will.

Activity

Draw a symbol to represent each of these lines of the Lord's Prayer.

hallowed be thy name . . .   thy will be done . . .   forgive us our trespasses . . .

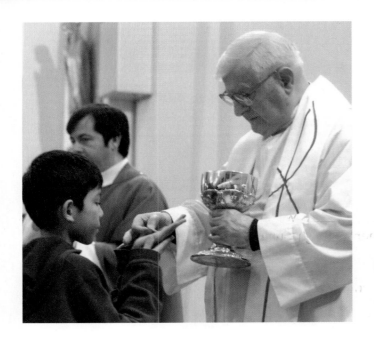

We show our trust that God hears us in the Lord's Prayer.

In the last four petitions of the Lord's Prayer, we pray with trust that God listens to us and responds to our needs. We pray for the graces of nourishment, mercy, and strength to live as children of God.

Give us this day our daily bread . . .
In the Sacrament of the Eucharist, we receive the living bread, Jesus himself. We become what we receive. We ask God to give us everything we need to live as Christ's disciples.

And forgive us our trespasses as we forgive those who trespass against us . . .
We pray for forgiveness of our own sins, and we pray for hearts that are merciful so that we can forgive others. All of us are in need of forgiveness, and all of us need to forgive. Forgiveness is a two-way street. We formally celebrate God's mercy and the forgiveness of sins in the Sacrament of Penance and Reconciliation.

And lead us not into temptation . . .
The temptations that we face every day try to convince us that there is something better than God's way. In the Lord's Prayer, we ask God to lead us away from situations and choices that try to pull us away from his love. The Sacrament of Confirmation, with the graces and gifts of the Holy Spirit it confers, strengthens us to avoid temptation and follow Jesus more closely.

But deliver us from evil . . .
Evil is real. The forces of evil work hard to distract us, to turn us away from God. But there is no power stronger than that of Jesus. By Jesus' Death and Resurrection, God's love has overcome evil. Regular participation in the Sacrament of the Eucharist and the Sacrament of Penance and Reconciliation helps us resist evil and live in God's love.

Partners in Faith

Saint John Neumann

Saint John Neumann arrived in America with the clothes on his back and one dollar. He had hoped to be ordained in his native Bohemia—part of what we now call the Czech Republic—but there were too many priests in that country. Three weeks after coming to America, John was ordained as a priest and began to work with German immigrants. Saint John helped found the first Catholic school system in the United States.

 Learn more about the life of Saint John Neumann.

Faith Word

Kingdom of God

☑ Show What You Know

Choose the correct term to complete the sentences.

1. When we pray the _____ , we are united
with God and Jesus, his Son, and with each other through our Baptism.
Lord's Prayer | Baptismal Promises

2. God's reign of peace, justice, and love is called the _____ .
Priesthood of God | Kingdom of God

3. In the last four _____ of the Lord's Prayer,
we pray with trust that God listens to us and responds to our needs.
petitions | psalms

Live Your Faith

• What are you doing now to help build up the Kingdom of God?

_____

_____

_____

_____

_____

_____

_____

Why do we ask God to "lead us not into temptation"? What strength does
God give you to avoid temptation?

_____

_____

_____

_____

_____

_____

_____

_____

_____

Mini-Task

Showing respect for others, even if we disagree with them or don't like them, is an essential part of being a good member of society and a true Christian. It is easy to say or share mean or degrading things about others, especially online when we may not face immediate consequences. How you treat others is a reflection of your character. The Lord's Prayer reminds us to treat one another with compassion and mercy, which are a foundation for being respectful.

On the lines below, write what you would do to show respect.

When I disagree with someone:

_____

_____

_____

When I don't like someone:

_____

_____

_____

When someone is different or doesn't fit in:

_____

_____

_____

 Want to do more? Go to your Portfolio to continue this activity.

 At Home

Pray the Our Father slowly together as a family. Ask each family member to share a word or phrase from the prayer that stood out to her or him.

✠ Liturgical Calendar

Liturgical calendar wheel showing: Easter, Triduum, Lent, Ordinary Time, Christmas, Advent, Ordinary Time, with months JAN–DEC and the EQUATOR marked across the center globe.

In the liturgical year, the date of Easter Sunday, the celebration of our Lord's Resurrection, depends each year on the spring equinox and the rising of the full moon. Easter Sunday follows the full moon after the spring equinox. The spring equinox is the day on which the sun crosses the equator, making day and night of equal length everywhere. Thus, the timing of Easter Sunday reminds us that our Lord's Resurrection brings light to our darkness.

Astronomers can calculate the date of the spring equinox. Looking at their calculations, we find that Easter Sunday is always between March 22 and April 25. Using the date for Easter Sunday, each year's unique liturgical calendar can be determined.

185

Unit Prayer

Leader: Saint Ignatius of Loyola taught that it is more important that we show our love for God by the way we live—that our deeds mean more than our words. Let us listen to how Jesus' love is shown to us today.

Listen to the stories of missionary disciples in our midst.

Let us pray:
Jesus, at Mass we are given all the tools that we need to be your disciples. It is there we are taught by your Word, fed by your Body and Blood, and sent to show the world that we love you by the way we live. Through each season of the Church year, we experience a different way to know of your love.

For Advent and Christmas, when we learn to wait for your coming and celebrate your birth in our hearts,

All: we bring your love to the world.

Leader: For Lent and Triduum, when we learn how to love by your Word, your life, and your Death and Resurrection,

All: we bring your love to the world.

Leader: For Easter, when the words of the prophets were fulfilled by your rising from the dead,

All: we bring your love to the world.

Leader: For Pentecost, when we are filled with the Holy Spirit, sending us forth to live as you have loved us,

All: we bring your love to the world.

Leader: For Ordinary Time, when we learn how to live your commands, showing the world in deed more than word of your love for us all,

All: we bring your love to the world.

Leader: Let us offer each other a sign of peace.

End the Unit Prayer by singing the song for this unit.

Unit Song: "We Are Called," David Haas

Missionary Discipleship

When have you been able to show someone how much God loves him or her? How did it feel? When has someone shown God's love to you? How did it feel?

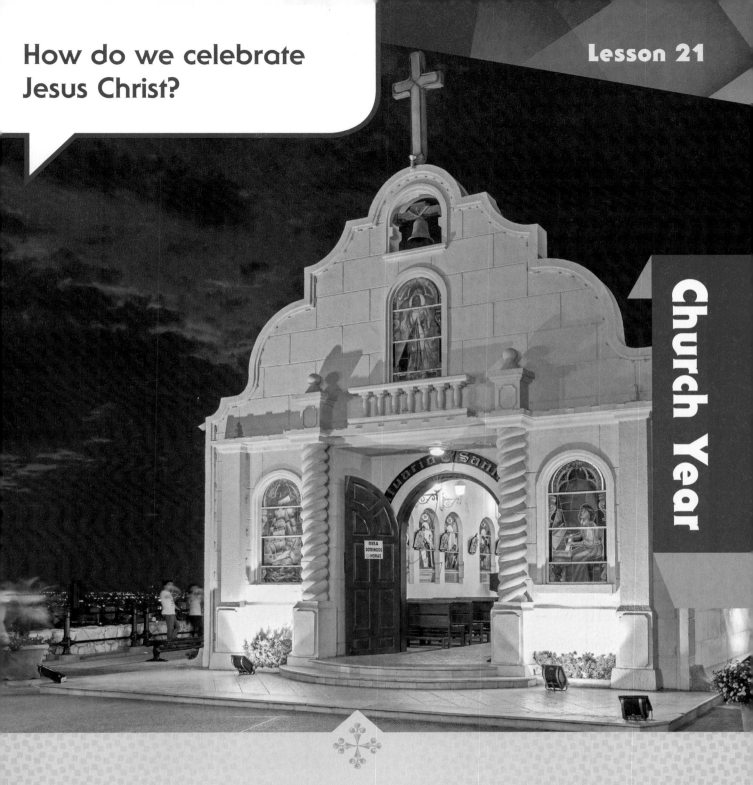

How do we celebrate Jesus Christ?

Church Year

"Pray . . . that God may open a door to us for the word, to speak of the mystery of Christ."

Colossians 4:3

Gathering Prayer

Leader: The Church year guides our celebrations of Jesus through different seasons and feasts. Each season focuses on a different aspect of the Paschal Mystery, yet all direct our focus toward the life, work, and love of Jesus Christ. We listen to the Scripture readings of all Christ did for us and learn from his example in all things.

We praise you, O God, for the life, work, and love of your Son, Jesus.

All: We praise you, O God, for the life, work, and love of your Son, Jesus.

Leader: In Advent, we prepare our hearts for the gift of Jesus Christ and the hope of his return in glory.

All: We praise you, O God, for the life, work, and love of your Son, Jesus.

Leader: At Christmas, we celebrate the infant King, Jesus, who was born for us and would die for us.

All: We praise you, O God, for the life, work, and love of your Son, Jesus.

Leader: During Lent, we ask Jesus Christ to help us turn our hearts back toward you, O God, and we give thanks for the gift of Christ's life and Death.

All: We praise you, O God, for the life, work, and love of your Son, Jesus.

Leader: The three holy days of the Easter Triduum bring us closer to God and make us more aware of Jesus' sacrifice for us, as we remember Jesus' Passion, Death, and Resurrection.

All: We praise you, O God, for the life, work, and love of your Son, Jesus.

Leader: In the joyful season of Easter, we celebrate that Christ is risen from the dead. His rising brings us hope that we, too, will live forever with God in heaven. Alleluia, alleluia!

All: We praise you, O God, for the life, work, and love of your Son, Jesus.

Leader: All year we learn from Jesus Christ and aim to live in his love and show that love to the world.

All: We praise you, O God, for the life, work, and love of your Son, Jesus.

Activity

Mind maps can help us understand ideas. In groups, create a mind map about one of the seasons of the liturgical year. Choose one season and write that season's name at the center of your map. Then, create your map by drawing lines from the center to other sections where you write words that come to mind when you think of that season. Circle the one word in your map that means the most to the entire group. Share your mind map with the other groups. Combine the seven words from all groups into one mind map to post at the front of the classroom.

The liturgical year celebrates God's saving work through his divine Son, Jesus.

During the liturgical year, the Church recalls and celebrates the whole mystery of Christ. We recall and celebrate God's work of salvation through the different feasts and seasons. All the seasons are united, because each season reveals the one mystery of Christ.

The high point of the liturgical year is Christ's Passion, Death, Resurrection, and Ascension. This is called the Paschal Mystery.

There are signs that point to the Paschal Mystery in every season. During Ordinary Time, Jesus tells his followers to take up their crosses. During Lent, Jesus predicts his Passion, and the story of the Transfiguration is like a preview of the Resurrection. The *Paschal* or Easter Triduum, the highest point of the year, remembers in a special way the life, Passion, Death, and Resurrection of Jesus Christ.

Even during Christmas, we have signs of the Paschal Mystery. The aromatic spices brought by the magi are used for burial. Yet the gold and frankincense they bring show that Jesus will be victorious as Lord and God.

The Paschal Mystery is what we celebrate in the Eucharist. The dying and rising of Jesus is made present to us in the Mass. We participate in it there. When we were baptized, we entered into this mystery. We died to sin and rose to a new life in Jesus. When we celebrate the Eucharist and receive Holy Communion, the Holy Spirit renews the life of God within us.

Sunday is the original feast day. It is the Lord's Day and the most appropriate day for celebrating the Eucharist. Sunday is the Lord's Day because it is the day of Jesus' Resurrection. Because of this, every Sunday is considered a "little Easter."

We keep Sunday holy by attending Mass, spending time with our families, and dedicating time to rest and care for ourselves and others.

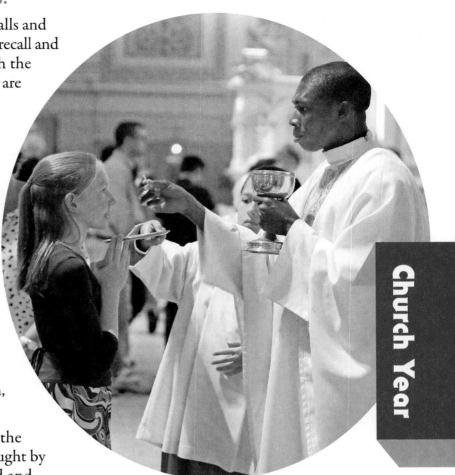

Church Year

Did You Know?

 The Paschal Mystery is the focus of the liturgy.

Activity

Form small groups to discuss the Church's seasons and the Paschal Mystery. Have each person in your group choose one season of the liturgical year and describe that season's connection to the Paschal Mystery.

Church Year Prayer Ritual

 "The Lord Has Done Great Things for Us,"
Jaime Cortez

Leader: In the name of the Father, and of the Son, and of the Holy Spirit. Amen.

The liturgical year is made up of the seasons of Advent, Christmas, Ordinary Time, Lent, Triduum, and Easter. We experience this calendar most clearly when we gather for Mass each week. Through the Liturgy of the Word and the Liturgy of the Eucharist, we encounter the living Christ in the Word of God and in the Eucharist. The Word of God and the Eucharist together guide and transform us so that we may be Christ to one another.

The Church teaches that we also encounter Christ in each other. One of the ways that we celebrate Christ alive in each other while at Mass is to pray and sing together.

In Advent, we ask Jesus to help us prepare a place in our hearts for his return and birth at Christmas. Prepare a place in our hearts, O Lord.

All: Prepare a place in our hearts, O Lord.

Reader 1: At Christmas, we celebrate the birth of our Lord, Jesus, alive in our hearts!

All: O Lord, help us to celebrate the birth of your Son with wonder and awe.

Reader 2: In Ordinary Time, we listen to Jesus teach us how to love God and one another in his many parables. We ask him to help us listen to his Word with open hearts and minds.

All: O Lord, help us to listen to your Word with open hearts and minds.

Reader 3: In the season of Lent, we make time for Jesus by prayer, fasting, and abstinence, and gifts of charity. We use this season to focus on Christ's love for us all and on our response to his call to love one another as God has loved us.

All: Help us to love one another as God has loved us.

Leader: The liturgies of the Easter Triduum are Holy Thursday, Good Friday, and the Easter liturgies. We first celebrate the Last Supper, when Jesus took bread and wine and gave us his Body and Blood. On Good Friday, we remember the Death of Jesus on the Cross. At the Easter Vigil and on Easter Sunday, we celebrate Jesus' Resurrection and his victory over sin and death.

All: Let all creation lift its voice in praise!

Reader 1: During the joyful season of Easter, we celebrate Jesus' Resurrection from the dead. Christ came to die for us and to rise from death, banishing all sin and darkness from our lives.

We are an Easter people who no longer live in darkness and sin but live in the light of Easter!

All: Alleluia, alleluia, alleluia!

Reader 2: And, finally, on the great feast of Pentecost, we receive the Holy Spirit of God to go out into the world and spread the Good News of Jesus Christ. We celebrate the manifestation of the Church!

All: Come, Holy Spirit, and renew the face of the earth.

Reader 3: As we pass around this candle, let us ask God to help us live in the light of his Son, Jesus, throughout the liturgical year.

(Pass around an unlit candle. When all have held the candle, pray.)

Leader: The light of Christ shines in us throughout the year. Amen. Alleluia!

All: Amen. Alleluia!

Church Year

How is Christ a part of my life all year long?

Mini-Task

The seasons of the liturgical year help us remember and celebrate the events of the Paschal Mystery: the life, Passion, Death, and Resurrection of Christ. Christ is the center of our life and Catholic faith. He is present in all of the Church's sacraments.

You will learn about the seasons of the liturgical year. In every season the Church celebrates and remembers Christ and his presence in the Church today.

As you learn and experience each season, you will compare and connect it to important events in your life. Begin the activity by comparing and connecting the liturgical year to your year. What are the ways the Church celebrates each liturgical season (such as Advent, Christmas, Lent, Triduum, Easter, and Ordinary Time)? How do you celebrate these seasons with your family? How does your celebration of the season connect with the Church's celebration? How does it differ?

Compare and Contrast Chart Graphic Organizer

1. _____   2. _____

How are they alike?

How are they different?

 Want to do more? Go to your Portfolio to continue this activity.

Together, brainstorm ways that you can make Sunday a special day of the week for your family, even if family members have different responsibilities on that day.

Why does Jesus come to save us?

Advent

"*Whoever is in Christ is a new creation: the old things have passed away; behold, new things have come.*"

2 Corinthians 5:17

Gathering Prayer

Leader: Bless us this Advent as we wait in joyful hope for your coming to us. We celebrate this season by preparing our homes and our hearts. Each Sunday, another candle in the Advent wreath is lit. On the Fourth Sunday of Advent, the four lights for each week give off your light.

We wait in joyful hope for your coming to us, Lord Jesus.

All: We wait in joyful hope for your coming to us, Lord Jesus.

Leader: "A voice proclaims:

In the wilderness prepare the way of the LORD!" (Isaiah 40:3).

All: We wait in joyful hope for your coming to us, Lord Jesus.

Leader: "Every valley shall be lifted up,
every mountain and hill made low" (Isaiah 40:4).

All: We wait in joyful hope for your coming to us, Lord Jesus.

Leader: "Then the glory of the LORD shall be revealed,
and all flesh shall see it together" (Isaiah 40:5).

All: We wait in joyful hope for your coming to us, Lord Jesus.

Leader: Lord Jesus, prepare in our hearts the path of your return.

All: We wait in joyful hope for your coming to us, Lord Jesus.

Activity

The Church celebrates Christmas on December 25. But in many places the "holiday spirit" begins much earlier. As a class, discuss ways you can take part in the holiday spirit while still keeping Advent as a time of penance and prayer.

Our hearts look forward to the coming of Christ.

In the Nicene Creed, we profess our faith. We say that we believe that Jesus "will come again in glory."

The season of Advent is that time of the year when we remember and celebrate the fact that Jesus Christ will come again in glory. No one knows the day or the hour when Christ will return. Therefore, we must be ready to meet him whenever he comes, our hearts filled with wonder, love, and praise.

Many people are fearful when they think about the end of the world. It will be a time of great turmoil and destruction. Yet believers can be confident that Christ will gather all who believe in him together and protect us from all harm. We need never be afraid.

We know that the world is not eternal. It had a beginning, and it will have an end. The account of creation assures us that God is the source of the world's beginning. The New Testament assures us that when Jesus comes again in glory, he will reign over all things. The end of time, as well as its beginning, is in the safe hands of the Creator, God the Father.

Advent marks the beginning of the liturgical year. Yet the First Sunday of Advent emphasizes the coming of Jesus at the end of time. Does it not seem strange that at the beginning of a new liturgical year, the readings for Mass speak about the end of the world?

The liturgy reminds us every year that we are on a journey together. Advent is the start of each new liturgical cycle. In Advent, we look ahead, with joy-filled hope, to the birth of Jesus Christ and remembering his coming in glory that is to come at the end of time. His birth and second coming are good news for all God's faithful.

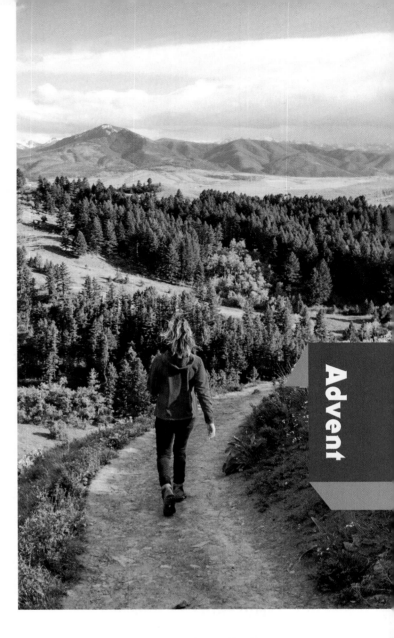

Advent

Did You Know?

Jesus is here—be not afraid.

Activity

Advent means "coming." Ask two or three friends why Advent in the Church does not mean waiting for Christmas but waiting for the coming of Jesus. Summarize their answers and present your results to the class.

Readers Theater

Joseph's Dream

Roles:
Narrator 1, Narrator 2, Narrator 3, Joseph, Angel

Joseph faces a difficult decision when he finds out that Mary is pregnant.
An angel helps him to decide.

Narrator 1: This is an account of how Joseph became aware that Mary would give birth to Jesus. It was during the time when Joseph and Mary were betrothed.

Narrator 2: "Betrothed" was the first stage of marriage during the time of Joseph and Mary. It was like being engaged.

Narrator 3: Mary was found to be with child through the Holy Spirit. Joseph did not yet fully understand what this all meant.

Joseph: I love Mary and want to protect her. But when people find out that she is pregnant and we are not yet married, she will be shamed. It would be better for her if I leave.

Narrator 1: As he was thinking of all of this, he fell into a deep sleep.

Narrator 2: Suddenly, an angel of the Lord appeared to him in a dream!

Angel: "Joseph, son of David, do not be afraid to take Mary your wife into your home. For it is through the holy Spirit that this child has been conceived in her. She will bear a son and you are to name him Jesus, because he will save his people from their sins" (Matthew 1:20–21).

Narrator 3: When Joseph woke up, he did all the angel of the Lord told him to do.

The Dream of Saint Joseph, 19th-century lithograph by Emile Beau

How do I look forward to the coming of Christ?

Mini-Task

Advent begins the liturgical year. During the season of Advent, we look forward to celebrating the birth of Jesus. Jesus, whose name means "God saves," is the long-awaited Savior. It is fitting that the first season of the liturgical year helps us to remember the hope that Jesus would bring to God's people.

Compare and connect the meaning and experience of Advent to an event in your life.

Compare and Contrast Chart Graphic Organizer

1. _____   2. _____

How are they alike?

_____
_____
_____
_____

How are they different?

_____
_____
_____
_____
_____
_____
_____

 Want to do more? Go to your Portfolio to continue this activity.

 At Home

Talk with your family about a family event or occasion you are looking forward to. Pray together that the beginning and end of this event or occasion will go well for your family.

Christmas

"And the Word became flesh . . . and we saw his glory."

John 1:14

Gathering Prayer

Leader: This Christmas, let us celebrate the gift of Jesus, the gift of love. As we gather at Mass to sing carols and hymns of the season, let us offer prayers of thanksgiving to God for the gift of Jesus, his Son. God loved us so much that he became one of us. Through Jesus we have come to know the love of God the Father.

Jesus, Prince of Peace, we give glory to your name!

All: Jesus, Prince of Peace, we give glory to your name!

Leader: Lord Jesus, you are Word Made Flesh. We give glory to your name!

All: Jesus, Prince of Peace, we give glory to your name!

Leader: Christ Jesus, you are Wonder-Counselor. We give glory to your name!

All: Jesus, Prince of Peace, we give glory to your name!

Leader: Lord Jesus, you are Light from Light, true God from true God!

All: Jesus, Prince of Peace, we give glory to your name!

Leader: Christ Jesus, you were begotten, not made, consubstantial with the Father!

All: Jesus, Prince of Peace, we give glory to your name!

Activity

The prayer above gives some names used to describe Jesus Christ. In groups, brainstorm ideas for what each name tells us about Jesus. Share with the whole group.

Name for Christ	What does this name tell us about Jesus?
Prince of Peace	
Word Made Flesh	
Wonder-Counselor	
Light from Light	

The Son of God, the Second Person of the Trinity, was present with the Father and the Holy Spirit even before creation. God has no beginning. Through the Incarnation, the Son of God became man.

The Incarnation strengthens Catholics in the belief that God works through the material world rather than remaining far apart from it. The physical world, although imperfect and full of suffering, is still a place to encounter God's presence.

The Incarnation shows us that we must respect everyone. Because God's Son took on human flesh and dignified it by becoming one of us, we know that our own bodies and those of others are made in the image of God.

At Christmas we celebrate the Incarnation.

The Gospel according to John does not tell the story of Jesus' birth as it is told in the Gospels of Matthew or Luke. Instead, John offers a beautiful, poetic hymn to the Incarnation. He writes:

"In the beginning was the Word,
　　and the Word was with God,
　　and the Word was God." (John 1:1)

John goes on to talk about the Son of God as "light" coming into the world. Finally, he says:

"And the Word became flesh
　　and made his dwelling among us,
　　and we saw his glory,
　　the glory as of the Father's only Son,
　　full of grace and truth." (John 1:14)

This passage, which is the reading for the Mass During the Day on Christmas, tells us something very important about what we celebrate.

This Scripture reading shows that Christmas is, above all, the feast of the Incarnation: that Jesus, the Son of God, was born like us in all things but sin. The Word was made flesh. God's Word, in an act of grace, became flesh through the Virgin Mary.

Did You Know?

 God uses physical things to explain spiritual mysteries.

Activity

The word *incarnation* comes from the Latin, meaning "to make flesh." It refers to Jesus, the Second Person of the Trinity, taking on a human nature. List three reasons why it is important to our faith that the Son of God became man.

_____

_____

_____

Using these reasons, write a brief poem, paragraph, or song to share with the group. If you write a song, you might want to use a Christmas carol for the melody.

Readers Theater

Shepherds at the Birth of Jesus

Roles:
Narrator 1, Narrator 2, Narrator 3, Narrator 4,
Shepherds (2 or 3), Heavenly Host, Angel
Glory to God in the highest.

Narrator 1: In those days a decree went out from Caesar Augustus declaring that the whole world should be enrolled.

Narrator 2: This meant that all family members had to travel to their own town to be counted.

Narrator 3: So Mary, who was with child, and her husband, Joseph, went up from the town of Nazareth to the city of David called Bethlehem.

Narrator 4: Joseph was of the house and family of David.

Narrator 1: While Mary and Joseph were there, the time came for Mary to have her child, and she gave birth to Jesus.

Narrator 2: She wrapped him in swaddling clothes and laid him in a manger, because there was no room for them to stay at the inn.

Narrator 3: At the same time, shepherds who lived in fields outside Bethlehem were keeping watch on their sheep all night. All was quiet.

Narrator 4: Then suddenly an angel appeared to them. The glory of God shone all around them! The shepherds were very afraid.

Shepherds: What is happening?

Angel: "Do not be afraid; for behold, I proclaim to you good news of great joy that will be for all the people. For today in the city of David a savior has been born for you who is Messiah and Lord. And this will be a sign for you: you will find an infant wrapped in swaddling clothes and lying in a manger" (Luke 2:10–12).

Heavenly Host: "Glory to God in the highest
and on earth peace to those on whom his favor rests"
(Luke 2:14).

Narrator 1: The shepherds were amazed.

Narrator 2: They hurried to see this baby whom the angels
sang about.

Narrator 3: The shepherds went back to watching their sheep.

Narrator 4: But they wanted to tell everyone about the baby Jesus.

The Adoration of the Shepherds, 1534, by Lorenzo Lotto

Mini-Task

During the Christmas season, we celebrate that God became man in the Incarnation of Christ. Christmas is a time of peace and joy. It can be a time of healing for families and groups of people as we all celebrate the birth of Jesus.

Compare and connect the meaning and experience of Christmas to an event in your life. What and how do you celebrate in each?

Compare and Contrast Chart Graphic Organizer

1. _____

2. _____

How are they alike?

How are they different?

Want to do more? Go to your Portfolio to continue this activity.

Ask your family members to tell about some ways they see Jesus' presence in the world. Talk about ways you see his presence in one another.

How are we called to repentance today?

Lent

"He restores my soul.
He guides me along right paths
for the sake of his name."

Psalm 23:3

Gathering Prayer

Leader: The season of Lent is a time for us to prepare our hearts for the celebration of Christ's rising from the dead at Easter. We take this time in Lent to pray and fast, and to experience conversion. God's presence in his holy Word feeds our minds with wisdom and knowledge. The Real Presence of Jesus in his Body and Blood fills us with his love and strength. We experience conversion as we celebrate the Sacrament of Penance and Reconciliation. We reflect on the choices we have made and turn our hearts back toward God.

Lord Jesus, help us to listen to your Word with the ears of our hearts, that we may turn our hearts to you and live as your light in the world.

Create in me a clean heart, O God.

All: Create in me a clean heart, O God.

Leader: Lord Jesus, your Real Presence in the Eucharist is the food that feeds and strengthens us. Your light in us will shine for all to see.

Create in me a clean heart, O God.

All: Create in me a clean heart, O God.

Leader: Lord Jesus, forgive us our sins and celebrate with us the conversion of our hearts in the Sacrament of Penance and Reconciliation. Guide us to live so that others may recognize you in everything we do.

Create in me a clean heart, O God.

All: Create in me a clean heart, O God.

Activity

An examination of conscience can help us prepare for the Sacrament of Penance, but during the season of Lent, it can also help us see areas where we can improve on the good we want to do. Use the examination of conscience to choose some ways to be a better person during Lent.

Lent calls us to renewal.

Lent is a season in which we renew our faith. Just as Jesus went out into the desert and fasted for forty days to prepare for his mission, so we renew our commitment each year during the forty days of Lent.

We renew our faith, first of all, by following the three disciplines of Lent: prayer, fasting, and almsgiving. Our prayer, both personal prayer and communal prayer, should be especially earnest at this time.

During Lent, Catholics fast according to the rules of the Church on two days: Ash Wednesday and Good Friday. We abstain from meat on Fridays. But we might also practice self-denial by fasting at other times or by voluntarily giving up something we enjoy. Fasting is the practice of eating smaller meals, mostly during Lent, as a sign of our need for God and our dependence on God. In the United States, those who are between 18 and 59 years of age are invited to fast and abstain from eating meat. Almsgiving, which means giving to the poor, is something we should do in all seasons, but during Lent we should be especially generous.

The other way we renew our faith is through the Sacrament of the Eucharist and the Sacrament of Penance and Reconciliation. The Eucharist is a sacrament that strengthens us in holiness. It cleanses us from our less serious sins and renews the life of God within us. Every time we say "amen" when we receive Holy Communion, we are saying "yes" to the life God has given us in Baptism. The Eucharist commits us to live as followers of Jesus.

The Sacrament of Penance and Reconciliation is the other sacrament that renews our faith in a special way. By confessing our sins and receiving God's forgiveness through absolution, we are freed from our sins and strengthened to resist temptation.

In the Easter liturgy, we will renew our baptismal promises. We promise to reject Satan, and we profess our faith. We take the whole season of Lent to prepare for this renewal at Easter so that our words will not be empty promises but a true expression of faith.

Did You Know?

Our Lenten fasting reminds us of Jesus' fasting in the desert.

Activity

English speakers refer to this season of the Church year as Lent, from the Old English word *lencten* for "springtime." Most of the rest of the world calls the season by different names. Latin-based languages use words that mean "fortieth," since the Lenten season is forty days long. Other languages use words that mean "fasting time" or "great fast." Think about what the Church remembers and does during Lent. As a group, talk about which name for this season makes the most sense to you given what happens during this time.

Lent Prayer Ritual

 "Your Grace Is Enough,"
Matt Maher

Leader: In the name of the Father, and of the Son, and of the Holy Spirit. Amen.

The season of Lent is a time for us to prepare our hearts for Jesus' Death and Resurrection. The Sign of the Cross that we just made reminds us that we are a people who is loved by a God who became one of us only to die and then rise from death. Just as Jesus died on the Cross, we carry the Cross of Jesus in our own lives and are reminded that we are never alone; Jesus is always with us when we are carrying our own crosses. As we pray, let us pass this cross among us.

Our eyes are always on you, O Lord.

All: Our eyes are always on you, O Lord.

Reader 1: In you, O Lord, we place all our trust and hope, because of your goodness.

All: Our eyes are always on you, O Lord.

Reader 2: Remember your love, O Lord, that you have shown from of old.

All: Our eyes are always on you, O Lord.

Reader 3: Do not let us down; protect us from our foes. Turn to me, O Lord.

All: Our eyes are always on you, O Lord.

Reader 1: What joy and peace is life in you; you alone give us joy and peace. You alone are Lord!

All: Our eyes are always on you, O Lord.

Reader 2: We now ask God to hear our own prayers as we take the cross of Jesus and pray.

(Hold the cross and offer a brief prayer in your own words. Then, hand on the cross to the next person. After each prayer, all pray:)

All: Our eyes are always on you.

Leader: O Lord, we ask you to hear our prayers and lift up the needs of everyone that we prayed for today.

Let us close with the Lord's Prayer. Our Father . . .

Lent

How do I renew my faith during Lent?

Mini-Task

Lent is a time to focus our thoughts on how we can better live as Christ's disciples. We perform acts of self-denial and renew our faith. We get ready to celebrate the wonder of Christ's Resurrection at Easter.

Compare and connect the meaning and experience of Lent with an event in your life. What and how do you celebrate in each?

Compare and Contrast Chart Graphic Organizer

1. _____   2. _____

How are they alike?

_____
_____
_____
_____

How are they different?

Want to do more? Go to your Portfolio to continue this activity.

At Home

As a family, talk about how spring is a time of renewal in nature. Talk about how renewal is a fresh start. Then talk about Lent as a time of renewal for Christians. Have family members choose ways they can renew their faith this week.

Triduum

"Your light must shine before others, that they may see your good deeds and glorify your heavenly Father."

Matthew 5:16

Gathering Prayer

Leader: During Holy Week, Lent ends and we celebrate the Triduum: the Passion, Death and Resurrection of Jesus, believing that one day we, too, will be with God in heaven. Every knee shall bow at the name of Jesus! Glory and praise to you, Lord Jesus Christ.

All: Glory and praise to you, Lord Jesus Christ.

Leader: On Holy Thursday, we celebrate the gift of the Eucharist. Thank you, Jesus, for teaching us how to love God through the gift of the Eucharist. Glory and praise to you, Lord Jesus Christ.

All: Glory and praise to you, Lord Jesus Christ.

Leader: On Good Friday, we remember how much you loved us by dying on the Cross. We know how much you suffered for us. Glory and praise to you, Lord Jesus Christ.

All: Glory and praise to you, Lord Jesus Christ.

Leader: Lord Jesus, just as you promised, you rose from the dead on Easter. Let us praise you by living as people of light—as Easter people.

All: Glory and praise to you, Lord Jesus Christ.

Leader: As we make the Sign of the Cross, help us remember how much Jesus loves us by giving his life for us on the Cross.

All: In the name of the Father, and the Son, and the Holy Spirit. Amen.

Glory and praise to you, Lord Jesus Christ.

Activity

Triduum comes from the Latin word meaning "three days." Another word that contains "tri" is Trinity. What role does each member of the Blessed Trinity play during the Triduum? Fill in the chart, and then discuss your thoughts with your group.

Father	
Son	
Holy Spirit	

The Triduum is the high point of the liturgical year.

The Triduum is celebrated over three days. It begins with the Mass of the Lord's Supper on Holy Thursday night. It continues with the celebration of the Passion of the Lord on Good Friday. On Holy Saturday night, we celebrate the Easter Vigil, the greatest of all solemnities. The Triduum ends on Easter Sunday night.

The Triduum celebrates the Death and Resurrection of the Lord, which is the central mystery of the Christian faith. The Easter Vigil is the high point of the Triduum. We move from darkness into light and from death to resurrection.

The Easter Vigil is an occasion for celebrating the Sacraments of Initiation. This celebration shows the connection between the Resurrection of Jesus Christ and the new life given in the sacraments. Members of the whole parish community renew their own baptismal promises.

The Paschal candle is lit from the Easter fire at the Vigil. The candle symbolizes the light of Christ. A candle lit from the Paschal candle is given to each of the newly baptized. The white garment worn by the newly baptized symbolizes their new identity in Christ. Through Baptism, we pass from sin and death to a new life of grace.

Did You Know?

 There are sacred times and spaces.

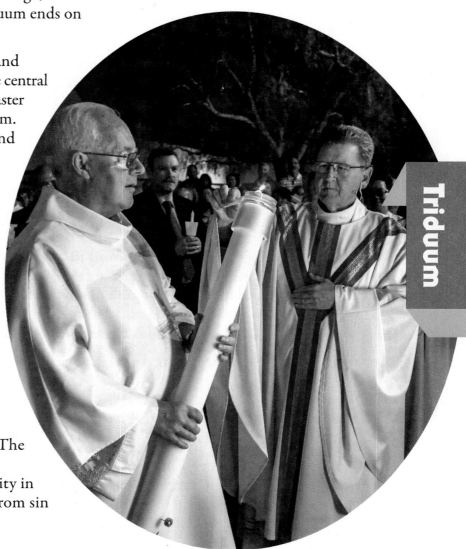

Triduum

Activity

Catholic churches have a candle or a special light that burns all the time alongside the tabernacle. The light reminds us of Jesus' divine presence in the Blessed Sacrament. It is called the tabernacle light. During the Easter Triduum, that light is put out. It is not lit again until Easter Sunday. Why do you think the light is put out during the Triduum? Interview several members of your group to get their ideas as well. Is there one reason you all agree on?

Triduum Prayer Ritual

"I Will Have Faith In You,"
Sarah Hart

Leader: In the name of the Father, and of the Son, and of the Holy Spirit. Amen.

At the end of the season of Lent, we celebrate the Easter Triduum for three days, with only one liturgy that begins with Holy Thursday, a night of service by our Lord and when he instituted the gift of Holy Communion. On Good Friday, the liturgy continues as we remember the Death of Jesus by listening to the story of his Passion and Crucifixion. On Holy Saturday, the liturgy continues as we begin in darkness, light the Easter candle, listen to the *Exsultet*, and celebrate the Resurrection of Jesus. When we celebrate the Triduum, we celebrate Christ's passing from this world back to the Father.

Let us listen to a Scripture reading from the Gospel of John (13:3–4, 12, 15).

Reader 1: "Fully aware that the Father had put everything into his power and that he had come from God and was returning to God, he rose from supper and took off his outer garments. He took a towel and tied it around his waist. . . . So when he had washed their feet [and] put his garments back on and reclined at table again, he said to them, 'Do you realize what I have done for you? . . . I have given you a model to follow, so that as I have done for you, you should also do.'"

Leader: Let us take a few minutes to think about this reading.

(*Silent reflection.*)

Reader 2: What do you think it would have been like to have your feet washed by Jesus? Do you think that some of the Apostles were upset or confused? How would you have felt?

Reader 3: At your Baptism, you were "commissioned" to go and live the Gospel, to wash each other's feet. That means each of us is called to care for one another and treat others with love. How will we respond to this call?

Leader: Where there are people in need, you are called to have a kind and loving heart. You are called to give yourself to help others.

All: Lord, give us kind and loving hearts.

Reader 1: We are called to help those who are sad and lonely, to show care and compassion.

All: Lord, show us how to show care and compassion in your name.

Reader 2: We are called to share the Word of God with those who have not heard it.

All: Lord, help us go out into the world and share the Good News, through our words and our actions.

Reader 3: Let us now ask God to hear our prayers for all the People of God, the Church, that we may wash the feet of others as Jesus did.

All: Lord, help us to love one another.

Reader 1: We pray for all on earth, that we treat each other as God's creation, made in his image and likeness.

All: Lord, help us to love one another.

Reader 2: We pray for our parish, that it be a light to the community that it is in, always living as Christ taught: "Love one another as I have loved you."

All: Lord, help us to love one another.

Reader 3: We pray for our families, that we might live in the light of Christ and celebrate his love in all we say and do.

All: Lord, help us to love one another.

Leader: We now pray for all of your own intentions . . .

All: (*Say: "Lord, help us to love one another" after each spoken intention.*)

Leader: Let us pray as Jesus taught us: Our Father, . . .

How do you pray during the Triduum?

Mini-Task

The three holy days of the Easter Triduum are a time to connect what we do in the Church now to how Jesus shared his love and life with his followers during the last days of his life on earth. We remember the gifts we receive from Christ in the sacraments. We get closer and closer to the mystery of Jesus' Resurrection at Easter.

Compare and connect the meaning and experience of the Triduum with an event in your life. What and how do you celebrate in each?

Compare and Contrast Chart Graphic Organizer

1. _____

2. _____

How are they alike?

_____
_____
_____
_____

How are they different?

_____
_____
_____
_____
_____
_____
_____
_____

 Want to do more? Go to your Portfolio to continue this activity.

 At Home

During your evening prayers tonight, turn off the lights in your home. Illuminate your prayer time with candles or small flashlights. Talk with your family about how the light of Christ lights your way, every day.

How is the Risen Jesus present in his Church?

Easter

"Were not our hearts burning [within us] while he spoke to us on the way and opened the scriptures to us?"

Luke 24:32

Gathering Prayer

Leader: The song of Easter is "Alleluia!" Because we are a people of light, we are Easter people. "Alleluia" is our song. The song of Easter is meant to be sung loudly and lively throughout this joy-filled time of light, water, hope, and sacrament. As we gather each Sunday at Mass to celebrate Christ's Resurrection, we are nourished by the rituals of the Church during this beautiful season.

Like flowers blooming in the spring, so does the love of God bloom in our hearts. Jesus lives, alleluia, alleluia!

All: Jesus lives, alleluia, alleluia!

Leader: Let us be the light of Christ in the world.

All: Jesus lives, alleluia, alleluia!

Leader: Let us be a river of hope to all people.

All: Jesus lives, alleluia, alleluia!

Leader: Let us be the eyes and hands of Christ.

All: Jesus lives, alleluia, alleluia!

Leader: Jesus lives, alleluia, alleluia!

All: Jesus lives, alleluia, alleluia!

Activity

The disciples met Jesus on the road to Emmaus (see Luke 24:13–35) but did not recognize him at first. Jesus was a stranger to them. Imagine that you were one of the disciples who met Jesus on the way to Emmaus. Get into groups to discuss these questions:

How would you explain to the stranger what had happened to Jesus?

What would you say and do when Jesus broke the bread during your meal?

What would you tell other people about what you had seen?

Share your thoughts with the whole group.

Jesus is with us at Easter and always.

On the Third Sunday of Easter each year, the Gospel reading tells a story of how the Risen Jesus appeared to his followers and ate with them. The Gospel that is read in Year A, Luke 24:13–35, may be the most special of these stories.

This reading tells about two disciples who met a stranger on the road to Emmaus. They talked with him as they walked along. His words inspired them. He seemed to understand everything.

It was only when the stranger came to supper with them, broke the bread, and said the blessing that the disciples realized this was Jesus! The Gospel says: "Their eyes were opened and they recognized him" (Luke 24:31). The disciples ran to tell everyone: Jesus is risen.

The Risen Lord continues to make his presence known today in the Eucharist. When we share his Body and Blood, the Risen Lord is truly present. The presence of Jesus in the Eucharist is a mystery. But through the power of the Holy Spirit, we know that Jesus is with us. The joy of Easter is part of every Eucharist.

Easter

Did You Know?

 The Risen Jesus is with us.

Activity

Work in groups to build a timeline of what happened on the first Easter. Write some of the things that happened, who was present, and what they did. Read Luke 24:1–49 for details. Use the list of events below to help you.

Cleopas and the other person go to the Apostles.

Jesus appears to his disciples.

Jesus breaks bread with Cleopas and another person.

Jesus rises from the dead.

Mary Magdalene, Joanna, and others go to the tomb.

Peter runs to the tomb.

The men tell the women Jesus had risen.

The women tell the Apostles.

Readers Theater

On the Road to Emmaus

Roles:
Narrator 1, Narrator 2, Narrator 3, Cleopas, Disciple, Jesus

Two disciples of Jesus have a most interesting encounter on the road to Emmaus.

Narrator 1: On the very same day that Peter ran to the tomb of Jesus and was amazed to find it empty, two of Jesus' disciples were walking to a village seven miles outside Jerusalem—a town called Emmaus.

Narrator 2: Both disciples were talking about the events that had occurred over the past several days. Jesus had been tried and convicted. He was made to carry a heavy cross to the place where he was crucified. Then he was buried in the tomb. A large rock was hauled in front to seal the tomb. And now the tomb was empty!

Narrator 3: Empty! The two men could not get over it. They talked about what might have happened. Had Jesus' body been stolen? How could the rock have been moved? It was so heavy. They debated all the facts. They did not pay much attention to the man who started walking alongside them.

Narrator 1: They did not recognize that the stranger was Jesus.

Jesus: "What are you discussing as you walk along?" (Luke 24:17)

Narrator 2: The two men stopped abruptly. They looked downward. Their faces looked so sad. One of the men, named Cleopas, answered the stranger.

Cleopas: "Are you the only visitor to Jerusalem who does not know of the things that have taken place there in these days?" (Luke 24:18)

Jesus: "What sort of things?" (Luke 24:19)

Disciple: "The things that happened to Jesus the Nazarene, who was a prophet mighty in deed and word before God and all the people" (Luke 24:19).

Narrator 2: The men continued to tell the stranger about the events of the last few days. They recounted the hope they had had that Jesus would be the one to redeem Israel. But it had been three days, and now Jesus was dead.

Narrator 3: But then the two men's faces changed expression. They talked about some women from their group who had told them astounding news! The women were at Jesus' tomb early that very morning. They did not find his body! Instead, they had seen a vision of angels who announced Jesus was alive!

Narrator 2: Then the stranger, whom the two men still did not recognize as Jesus, spoke to them.

Jesus: "Oh, how foolish you are! How slow of heart to believe all that the prophets spoke! Was it not necessary that the Messiah should suffer these things and enter into his glory?" (Luke 24:25–26)

Narrator 3: Jesus continued to explain the Scriptures to the two men. Presently, the village of Emmaus stood before them. The men thought the stranger was going on farther. The men urged him to stay with them, for night was approaching. So Jesus went and stayed with them.

Narrator 1: While Jesus was with the two men at table, he took bread, said the blessing, broke it, and gave it to them. Suddenly, the men's eyes were opened!

Cleopas and Disciple: You are Jesus!

Narrator 2: At that very moment, Jesus vanished.

Narrator 3: The two men were stunned. They looked at each other.

Cleopas and Disciple: "Were not our hearts burning [within us] while he spoke to us on the way and opened the scriptures to us?" (Luke 24:32)

Narrator 1: The two men hurried off into the night and walked all the way back to Jerusalem. They could not wait to tell the others what had happened to them. As they approached the others, they exclaimed to them.

Cleopas and Disciple: "The Lord has truly been raised!" (Luke 24:34)

Narrator 2: Then the two men told all about what happened on the road to Emmaus and how they had met the Risen Lord in the breaking of the bread.

In what ways has Jesus revealed himself to you?

Mini-Task

Easter is a time of joy and celebration in the Church. We celebrate the Resurrection of Christ and sing the "Alleluia" again. We are reminded of Christ's presence in the sacraments and our lives every day.

Compare and connect the meaning and experience of Easter with an event in your life. What and how do you celebrate in each?

Compare and Contrast Chart Graphic Organizer

1. _____   2. _____

How are they alike?

_____
_____
_____
_____

How are they different?

_____
_____
_____
_____
_____
_____
_____

 Want to do more? Go to your Portfolio to continue this activity.

Share a meal tonight or tomorrow morning with Jesus. As a family, prepare a simple meal and choose a prayer or blessing to pray before you eat. Thank God for both the meal and his presence in your family's life.

Who is the Holy Spirit?

Pentecost

*"But as for me, I am filled with power,
with the spirit of the LORD."*

Micah 3:8

Gathering Prayer

Leader: On the Feast of Pentecost, the mission of the Church was fully revealed. Filled with the Holy Spirit, the disciples were sent out into the world as living witnesses to the love and message of Jesus, our Savior and King. We, too, are filled with the Holy Spirit and sent out into the world to share the love of Christ in us. We ask the Holy Spirit of God to guide us in our journey.

Lord, send us your Spirit; let us be one in you.

All: Lord, send us your Spirit; let us be one in you.

Leader: Lord, send us out, one by one, in your Spirit. Renew the face of the earth.

All: Lord, send us your Spirit; let us be one in you.

Leader: Lord, we will bring the Spirit of your peace to the world.

All: Lord, send us your Spirit; let us be one in you.

Leader: Lord, we will bring hope to all those needing your peace, hope, and love.

All: Lord, send us your Spirit; let us be one in you.

Leader: Lord, your Spirit gives strength to be a light when there is darkness.

All: Lord, send us your Spirit; let us be one in you.

Activity

The Holy Spirit is sometimes represented as a dove. Create a word cloud about the Holy Spirit. Share your word cloud with a friend. If there is time, create a new word cloud together.

The gifts of the Holy Spirit are with us today.

On Pentecost Sunday, the Church celebrates the wonderful way in which the Holy Spirit fulfills the promises of Jesus and showers gifts on us.

Jesus promised that he would send the Holy Spirit. He called the Spirit the "Advocate," because the Holy Spirit is active on our behalf. God the Holy Spirit intercedes for and speaks to God the Father on our behalf. In the struggle against temptation, the Holy Spirit is always fighting on our side.

Jesus also spoke about the Holy Spirit as the "Paraclete," who would explain everything that Jesus did for our salvation. The Holy Spirit enlightens our minds so that we can see what is good and what is evil.

Throughout Easter, the liturgy tells the story of how the Holy Spirit influenced the early Church. These stories offer us great examples of how the Spirit helps us on our way. The gifts of the Spirit help us always to follow where the Holy Spirit leads. These gifts are: wisdom, understanding, knowledge, counsel, piety, fortitude, and fear of the Lord.

Pentecost summarizes and celebrates the whole Easter season that comes before it.

Pentecost

Did You Know?

 Pentecost is one of the most important feast days of the Church.

Activity

Jesus calls the Holy Spirit the "Advocate" and the "Paraclete." These titles remind us that the Holy Spirit is our helper. Write about a time when you experienced the Holy Spirit helping or teaching you. You might also write a prayer asking the Holy Spirit to help or teach you now.

_____

_____

_____

_____

_____

Readers Theater

Life in Community

Roles:
**Narrator 1, Narrator 2, Narrator 3, Onlooker 1,
Onlooker 2, Peter**

*After Pentecost, amazing things began to happen
to the early Christian community.*

Narrator 1: The time had passed when the Church revealed herself at Pentecost.

Narrator 2: Many remembered the day in Jerusalem when the Apostles and Jesus' mother, Mary, were in one place together. All would never forget the sound of the heavenly noise that was like a strong driving wind.

Narrator 3: Others recalled that there were tongues of fire that rested on each of the Apostles and that they were filled with the Holy Spirit.

Onlooker 1: That was the day Jesus' followers came out of where they were staying. Outside, the crowd was enormous, what with this loud noise. There were devout Jews from every nation.

Onlooker 2: There also were Parthians, Medes, and Elamites, inhabitants of Mesopotamia, Judea and Cappadocia, Pontus and Asia, Phrygia and Pamphylia, Egypt and the districts of Libya near Cyrene, as well as travelers from Rome. There were both Jews and converts to Judaism, Cretans and Arabs. Just about everyone from many nations was there.

Onlooker 1: Here we all were from different parts of the world, yet the Apostles were speaking to each group in its own language. We were astounded! "What does this mean?" (Acts of the Apostles 2:12)

Onlooker 2: Peter stood up and spoke.

Peter: "God raised this Jesus; of this we are all witnesses. . . . Therefore let the whole house of Israel know for certain that God has made him both Lord and Messiah, this Jesus whom you crucified" (Acts of the Apostles 2:32, 36).

Narrator 2: After Peter spoke, the crowd wanted to know what to do.

Peter: Repent and be baptized in the name of Jesus Christ.

Narrator 3: Thousands did. All received the gifts of the Holy Spirit.

Narrator 1: But Pentecost did not end there. Those early followers of Jesus Christ lived out their newfound faith in the Risen Lord. What a wonderful time it was! They spent time learning the teachings of the Apostles and telling others about Jesus. They developed communities in which daily life was devoted to the breaking of the bread. They lived out a deeply felt prayer life.

Narrator 2: Many sold their property and gave away their possessions to share with the community. They ate their meals with joy, praising God in the highest. Soon, their neighbors and even strangers began admiring their sincerity and good will.

Onlookers 1 and 2: "And every day the Lord added to their number those who were being saved" (Acts of the Apostles 2:47).

In what ways have you shared the Good News of Jesus Christ?

Mini-Task

Pentecost is a time to respond to the call of discipleship. We celebrate the Holy Spirit coming to the Apostles to strengthen and encourage them. We remember that we are called to the same mission they were given—to share the Good News of Christ to all the world.

Compare and connect the meaning and experience of Pentecost with an event in your life. What and how do you celebrate in each?

Compare and Contrast Chart Graphic Organizer

1. _____   2. _____

How are they alike?

_____
_____
_____
_____

How are they different?

_____
_____
_____
_____
_____

| | |
_____
_____
_____
_____
_____

 Want to do more? Go to your Portfolio to continue this activity.

 At Home

Talk with your family about teachers or advocates you have known who helped you. In your prayers, ask God to bless these people and their work.

How do we grow as Jesus' followers?

Ordinary Time

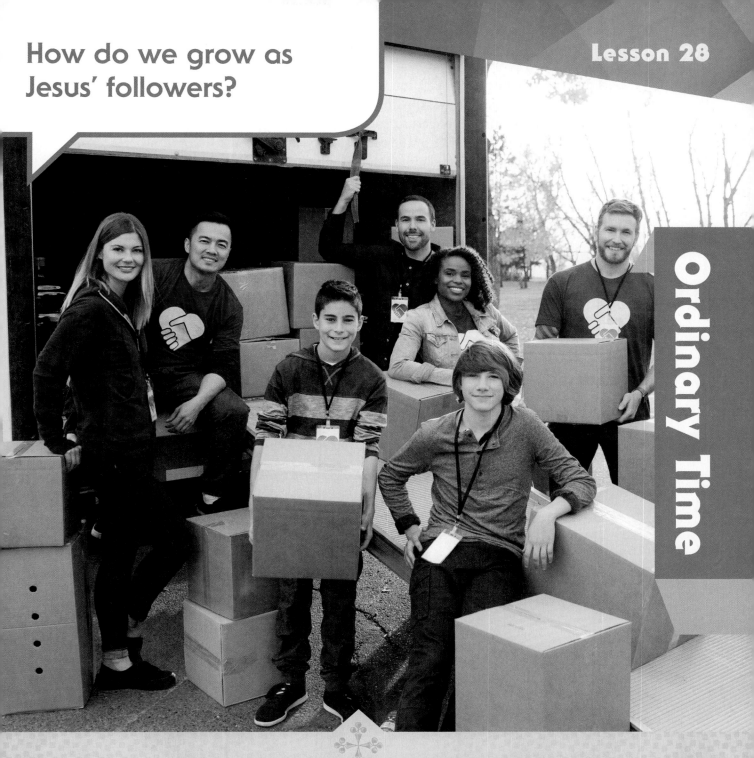

"Whoever is joined to the Lord becomes one spirit with him."

1 Corinthians 6:17

Gathering Prayer

Leader: Throughout the Church year, we learn about and experience God's love in many ways. Ordinary Time occurs after Christmas and Easter. It is the longest season of the Church year. During this season, we hear the stories of the early Church and how the first followers of Jesus began to change the world. Let us thank and praise God for the season of Ordinary Time and for the example of Jesus and the first disciples.

We are grateful for your Son and those who first believed in him.

All: O God, we are grateful for your Son and those who first believed in him.

Leader: For the Scripture accounts of the early Church; we are grateful for your Word in the Bible.

All: O God, we are grateful for your Word.

Leader: For the example of the disciples; we are grateful for their courage and strength.

All: O God, we are grateful for their courage and strength.

Leader: For the opportunity that this season gives us to learn from Jesus' example again and again; we are grateful for Ordinary Time.

All: O God, we are grateful for Ordinary Time.

Activity

Ordinary Time occurs in January and February, and in July through November. On the calendar, write some things that happen in your life during Ordinary Time. Write how you can use those events to grow in holiness. For example, you might celebrate your birthday by taking food to a shelter for the homeless.

Mary and the saints help us follow Jesus.

The season of Ordinary Time is a time for the Church to reflect on Christ's life and to grow in faithfulness to his teachings. Woven throughout the year is another calendar, the calendar of saints. The saints do not change our focus on Jesus; instead, they enrich it.

The saints offer us examples of holiness. They intercede for us before God. Devotion to the saints is part of the Church's life of prayer, which strengthens us in holiness.

Mary, the mother of Jesus, is the most important saint. We celebrate her Immaculate Conception—that from the moment of her conception, she was free of Original Sin. We celebrate Mary's birth and important events in her life, such as the Annunciation, the Visitation, and her Assumption into heaven. Several other days in the calendar honor Mary, too.

Aside from Mary, the only saint whose birth we celebrate is John the Baptist. Most other saints are celebrated on the anniversary of their death, which is considered their birthday into heaven.

We remember Mary and the saints in the Eucharistic Prayer at Mass. They join us in praising and thanking God for all that Christ has done.

Did You Know?

 Many saints are patron saints.

Activity

Saints are our role models. Have you ever thought about how you can be a role model, too? Think about ways you would like to be remembered for your faith. Maybe you enjoy singing or playing music in church. Maybe you love to compose prayers. On the lines below, write some ideas here about how you would like your faith to inspire others.

_____

_____

_____

Ordinary Time Prayer Ritual

 "We Are His People,"
Greg Walton

Leader: In the name of the Father, and of the Son, and of the Holy Spirit. Amen.

During the season of Ordinary Time, we follow in the footsteps of the early disciples. All who came to want to know more about Jesus would follow him as he went from town to town, teaching them about God's love for them and how to love God as Father.

He taught by using parables, or stories, each with a message of how to live with each other and ultimately how to love God by the way we treat each other. Let us listen now to a parable of Jesus that we hear during Ordinary Time.

Reader 1: "So Jesus said to them, 'Amen, Amen, I say to you, it was not Moses who gave the bread from heaven; my Father gives you the true bread from heaven. For the bread of God is that which comes down from heaven and gives life to the world.'

So they said to him, 'Sir, give us this bread always.' Jesus said to them, 'I am the bread of life; whoever comes to me will never hunger, and whoever believes in me will never thirst'" (John 6:32–35).

Reader 2: Let us take a few minutes to think about this reading.

Reader 3: What did Jesus mean when he said: "It was not Moses who gave the bread from heaven; my Father gives you the true bread from heaven" (John 6:32)?

Why is it important for us to receive the Eucharist? The symbol of the cross is often found on the host that we receive at Communion, a sign of Christ's love for us all.

As we pass around the cross, let us listen to the song "We Are His People."

(*Listen to the song.*)

Leader: Let us pray: For the gift of Jesus, the Bread of Life,

All: we are one Body in this one Lord.

Reader 1: For the living Body of Christ in our home, school, church, and in the world,

All: we are one Body in this one Lord.

Reader 2: For the gift of the season of Ordinary Time, a time to become disciples of Christ,

All: we are one Body in this one Lord.

Reader 3: We will now sing the song "We Are His People."

(*All sing.*)

Leader: As we close our ritual prayer, let us offer each other a sign of peace.

Mini-Task

Ordinary Time gives the Church a chance to remind ourselves of everything we have learned from Jesus. We connect his love and teachings with what we do here and now. We find joy and celebration in the everyday and make the ordinary extraordinary.

Compare and connect the meaning and experience of Ordinary Time with an event in your life. What and how do you celebrate in each?

Compare and Contrast Chart Graphic Organizer

1. _____   2. _____

How are they alike?

How are they different?

Want to do more? Go to your Portfolio to continue this activity.

Pray with the saints tonight as a family. You might pray the Rosary or choose a devotion to a particular saint. Afterward, talk together about why the saints are examples for your family.

Welcome

to your *Christ In Us* Sourcebook

Our Father

Our Father, who art in heaven,
hallowed be thy name;
thy kingdom come;
thy will be done on earth as
    it is in heaven.
Give us this day our daily bread;
and forgive us our trespasses
as we forgive those who
    trespass against us;
and lead us not into
temptation,
but deliver us from evil.
Amen.

Glory Be to the Father

Glory be to the Father
and to the Son
and to the Holy Spirit,
as it was in the beginning
is now, and ever shall be
world without end.
Amen.

Hail Mary

Hail Mary, full of grace,
the Lord is with you!
Blessed are you among women,
and blessed is the fruit of
    your womb, Jesus.
Holy Mary, Mother of God,
pray for us sinners,
now and at the hour of our death.
Amen.

Gloria

Glory to God in the highest,
and on earth peace to people of good will.
We praise you,
we bless you,
we adore you,
we glorify you,
we give you thanks for your great glory,
Lord God, heavenly King,
O God, almighty Father.
Lord Jesus Christ, Only Begotten Son,
Lord God, Lamb of God, Son of the Father,
you take away the sins of the world,
  have mercy on us;
you take away the sins of the world,
  receive our prayer;
you are seated at the right hand of the Father,
  have mercy on us.
For you alone are the Holy One,
you alone are the Lord,
you alone are the Most High,
Jesus Christ,
with the Holy Spirit,
in the glory of God the Father.
Amen.

Morning Offering

O Jesus, I offer you all my prayers, works,
joys, and sufferings of this day for all the
intentions of your most Sacred Heart. Amen.

Evening Prayer

Dear God, before I sleep
I want to thank you for this day,
so full of your kindness
and your joy.
I close my eyes to rest
safe in your loving care.
Amen.

Apostles' Creed

I believe in God, the Father almighty,
  Creator of heaven and earth,
and in Jesus Christ, his only Son,
  our Lord,
who was conceived by the Holy Spirit,
born of the Virgin Mary,
suffered under Pontius Pilate,
was crucified, died and was buried;
he descended into hell;
on the third day he rose again
from the dead;
he ascended into heaven,
and is seated at the right hand
  of God the Father almighty;
from there he will come to judge
  the living and the dead.
I believe in the Holy Spirit,
  the holy catholic Church,
  the communion of saints,
  the forgiveness of sins,
  the resurrection of the body,
  and life everlasting. Amen.

Act of Contrition

My God,
I am sorry for my sins with
  all my heart.
In choosing to do wrong
and failing to do good,
I have sinned against you
whom I should love above
  all things.
I firmly intend, with your help,
to do penance,
to sin no more,
and to avoid whatever
  leads me to sin.
Our Savior Jesus Christ
suffered and died for us.
In his name, my God,
  have mercy.
Amen.

Nicene Creed

I believe in one God,
  the Father almighty,
  maker of heaven and earth,
  of all things visible and invisible.
I believe in one Lord Jesus Christ,
  the Only Begotten Son of God,
  born of the Father before all ages.
God from God, Light from Light,
true God from true God,
begotten, not made, consubstantial
  with the Father;
through him all things were made.
For us men and for our salvation
  he came down from heaven,
and by the Holy Spirit
  was incarnate of the Virgin Mary,
  and became man.
For our sake he was crucified
  under Pontius Pilate,
he suffered death and was buried,
and rose again on the third day
  in accordance with the Scriptures.
He ascended into heaven
  and is seated at the right hand
  of the Father.
He will come again in glory to judge
  the living and the dead
  and his kingdom will have no end.
I believe in the Holy Spirit, the Lord,
  the giver of life,
who proceeds from the Father and the Son,
who with the Father and the Son is
  adored and glorified,
who has spoken through the prophets.
I believe in one, holy, catholic
  and apostolic Church.
I confess one Baptism for the
  forgiveness of sins
and I look forward to the resurrection of the
  dead and the life of the world to come.
Amen.

Grace Before Meals

Bless us, O Lord,
    and these your gifts
which we are about to receive
from your goodness.
Through Christ our Lord.
Amen.

Grace After Meals

We give you thanks, almighty God,
for these and all your gifts,
which we have received through
Christ our Lord.
Amen.

Memorare

Remember, most loving Virgin Mary,
never was it heard
that anyone who turned to you for help
was left unaided.
Inspired by this confidence,
though burdened by my sins,
I run to your protection
for you are my mother.
Mother of the Word of God,
do not despise my words of pleading
but be merciful and hear my prayer.
Amen.

The Canticle of Mary, The Magnificat

"My soul proclaims the greatness of the Lord;
    my spirit rejoices in God my savior.
For he has looked upon his handmaid's
lowliness;
    behold, from now on will all ages call me
    blessed.
The Mighty One has done great things for me,
    and holy is his name.
His mercy is from age to age
    to those who fear him.
He has shown might with his arm,
    dispersed the arrogant of mind and heart.
He has thrown down the rulers from their
thrones
    but lifted up the lowly.
The hungry he has filled with good things;
    the rich he has sent away empty.
He has helped Israel his servant,
    remembering his mercy,
according to his promise to our fathers,
    to Abraham and to his descendants forever."

Luke 1:46–55

Hail, Holy Queen

Hail, holy Queen, mother of mercy,
hail, our life, our sweetness, and our hope.
To you we cry, the children of Eve;
to you we send up our sighs,
mourning and weeping in this land of exile.
Turn, then, most gracious advocate,
your eyes of mercy toward us;
lead us home at last and show us
the blessed fruit of your womb,
Jesus: O clement, O loving, O sweet Virgin Mary.
Amen.

How to Pray the Rosary

Praying the Rosary creates a peaceful rhythm of prayer during which we can reflect on the mysteries of the Rosary, special times in the lives of Jesus and Mary. Follow the numbered steps to pray the Rosary.

1. Start with the Sign of the Cross.
2. Then pray the Apostles' Creed.
3. Pray an Our Father at every large bead.
4. Pray a Hail Mary at every small bead.
5. Pray a Glory Be to the Father after each set of small beads.
6. Pray the Hail, Holy Queen to end the Rosary.

Mysteries of the Rosary

Joyful Mysteries
1. The Annunciation
2. The Visitation
3. The Birth of Jesus
4. The Presentation of Jesus in the Temple
5. The Finding of Jesus in the Temple

Sorrowful Mysteries
1. The Agony in the Garden
2. The Scourging at the Pillar
3. The Crowning with Thorns
4. The Carrying of the Cross
5. The Crucifixion and Death of Jesus

Glorious Mysteries
1. The Resurrection
2. The Ascension
3. The Descent of the Holy Spirit upon the Apostles
4. The Assumption of Mary into Heaven
5. The Coronation of Mary as Queen of Heaven

The Mysteries of Light
1. Jesus' Baptism in the Jordan
2. The Miracle at the Wedding at Cana
3. Jesus Announces the Kingdom of God
4. The Transfiguration
5. The Institution of the Eucharist

1. **sanctuary** the part of the church that includes the altar and the ambo. The word *sanctuary* means "holy place."

2. **altar** the special table that is the center of the celebration of the Liturgy of the Eucharist, also called the Table of the Lord

3. **crucifix** a cross with a figure of Christ crucified, displayed in the sanctuary

4. **tabernacle** the special place in the church in which the Most Blessed Sacrament is placed in reserve

5. **sanctuary lamp** light or candle that is always lit near the tabernacle. It helps us to remember that Jesus is really present in the Most Blessed Sacrament.

6. **ambo** a sacred reading stand called the Table of the Word of God. The ambo is used only for proclamation of the Scripture in the liturgy.

7. **chalice** the special cup into which the priest pours grape wine that becomes the Blood of Christ during the Liturgy of the Eucharist

8. **paten** the special plate on which the priest places the wheat bread that becomes the Body of Christ during the Liturgy of the Eucharist

9. **cruets** small glass jars that contain the water and the grape wine used at Mass

10. **presider's chair** chair on which the priest who is celebrating Mass sits

11 **processional cross** cross with a figure of Christ crucified that is carried in the entrance procession and may also be carried during the Offertory procession and during recessional

12 **Paschal candle** a large candle that is blessed and lit every Easter. The lighted Paschal candle represents the Risen Christ among us. The flame of the Paschal candle is used to light baptismal candles.

13 **baptismal font or pool** contains the water that is blessed and used during the Sacrament of Baptism

14 **Stations of the Cross** fourteen pictures that help us to follow the footsteps of Jesus during his Passion and Death on the Cross

15 **Reconciliation Room or confessional** a separate space for celebrating the Sacrament of Penance and Reconciliation. This is where you meet the priest for individual confession and absolution. You may sit and talk to him face-to-face or kneel behind a screen.

16 **stained glass** colorful windows that may show saints or scenes from Scripture

17 **pews** where the assembly is seated during the celebration of Mass

18 **statue of Mary** image of the Mother of God, our greatest saint. Statues of other saints may also be found in the church.

Celebrating the Mass

Introductory Rites
Entrance Chant
Greeting
Penitential Act
Gloria
Collect

Do you and your family sometimes wonder what the Mass is really all about? Here is a simple guide that brings awareness to the greatest prayer of the Catholic Church—the celebration of the Eucharist, or Mass.

Take a closer look at how the Mass begins and ends and at the two parts of the Mass—the Liturgy of the Word and the Liturgy of the Eucharist. All our prayers of praise and thanksgiving form one single act of worship. Share the meaning of these sacred moments with your family.

We Gather . . .

What better way to begin our worship than with an entrance song and a procession of the priest and other ministers! This shows our unity, for together we are the Body of Christ—the Church—gathered in God's name. Watch as the priest and deacon kiss the altar and bow. For it is on the altar, the table of the Lord, that the sacrifice of Christ is made present. We remember and make present the work of salvation accomplished by Jesus through his life, Death, Resurrection, and Ascension into heaven.

Together we pray: "In the name of the Father, and of the Son, and of the Holy Spirit." God is with us. In God's presence, we confess that we are not perfect; we have sinned. We pray for God's mercy and ask for the prayers of the community and all the saints. In this way, we prepare ourselves—mind, heart, and soul—to participate in the sacred mysteries of the Mass.

On most Sundays we pray an ancient hymn called the *Gloria*, first sung by the angels at the birth of Christ: "Glory to God in the highest . . . / For you alone are the Lord, / you alone are the Most High, / Jesus Christ, / with the Holy Spirit, / in the glory of God the Father." This hymn of praise speaks of the mystery of the Trinity, the Triune God, in whose name we gather.

The priest then prays the Collect, the opening prayer that expresses the theme of the celebration and the needs and hopes of the assembly.

Liturgy of the Word

God placed in each of our hearts a desire to know him better. At Mass we are invited to actively listen to the Word of God. In Scripture, God speaks to us of the wonders of salvation and of his love for all creation. Yet God also has a special message for each individual who hears his Word. What might that be for you or for members of your family?

Our response after listening to the First Reading, usually from the Old Testament, and the Second Reading, from the New Testament, is "Thanks be to God." God's Word is not merely a collection of past events. God continues to act in our lives today; God's Word has the power to transform us.

Between these readings is the Responsorial Psalm, which can be spoken or sung. Jesus himself prayed the psalms, which express every kind of emotion, as well as what we desire from God. The psalms are beloved prayers of the Bible in which we ask the Lord for many things, such as insight, renewal, guidance, strength, and protection.

Our dialogue with God continues as we prepare to encounter Christ in the Gospel. Now, though, we are standing, singing *Alleluia*, or other words of praise. Standing is a sign of honor for the Gospel, the Good News of Jesus Christ. This is the high point of the Liturgy of the Word. Jesus Christ, our Savior, speaks to us—comforting, strengthening, and calling us to live as his disciples. As the priest or deacon introduces the Gospel (Matthew, Mark, Luke, or John) our bodies are at prayer, too. We trace a sign of the cross on our forehead, lips, and heart. In this way, we ask that God's Word be in our thoughts and in the words we speak, and that it take root in our hearts, moving us to praise and bless the Lord and to do good in the world.

The homily that follows is to help us understand what God's Word means and to remind us that we are not alone. God's Word is within us, guiding us and leading us to worship. The whole assembly then prays the Creed, stating aloud what we believe as members of the Church. In the Universal Prayer we pray for the needs of all God's people.

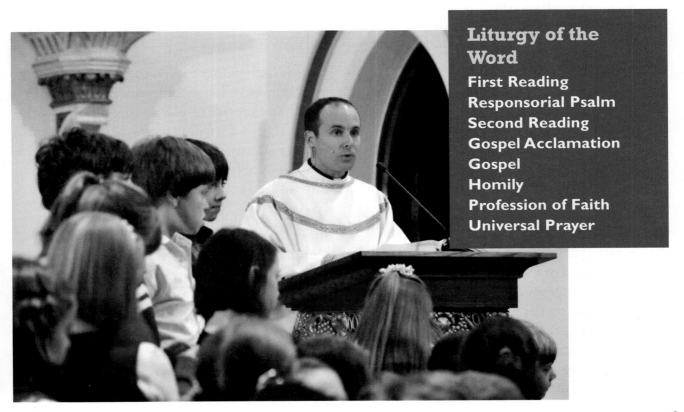

Liturgy of the Word

First Reading
Responsorial Psalm
Second Reading
Gospel Acclamation
Gospel
Homily
Profession of Faith
Universal Prayer

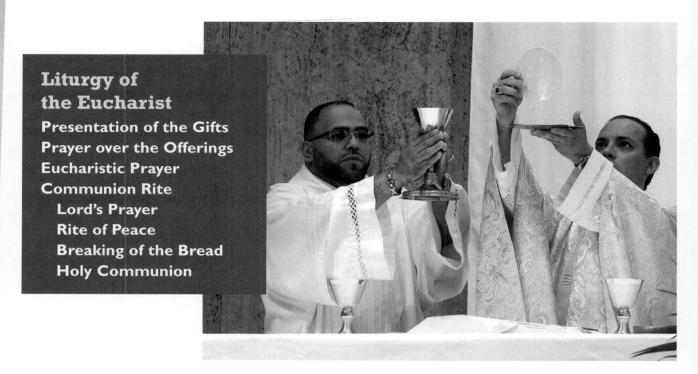

Liturgy of the Eucharist

At the heart of the entire liturgical celebration is the Liturgy of the Eucharist. It begins with the Presentation of the Gifts of bread and wine, and a Prayer over the Offerings. This is a symbolic expression of joining ourselves with the sacrifice of Christ. We should offer not only what is positive in our lives, but also our struggles and sorrows. In essence, we unite our whole selves—everything we are and hope to be—with the sacrifice of Christ.

Now is the time for the high point of the entire celebration—the Eucharistic Prayer. We are on our knees, in quiet reverence. The priest, in our name, thanks God for all his works of salvation. Our resounding response of praise is: "Holy, Holy, Holy Lord God of hosts. / Heaven and earth are full of your glory."

We have come to the very heart of the Mass—the changing of the bread and wine into the Body and Blood of Christ. What a beautiful mystery of faith. Jesus is our high priest, and Jesus is present on the altar under the appearances of bread and wine. This is what makes the celebration of Mass the "perfect" act of worship. Jesus is offering the sacrifice through the ministry of the priest *and* is the one being offered. Listen. You can hear Jesus' words, as the Apostles' heard so long ago: "THIS IS MY BODY, WHICH WILL BE GIVEN UP FOR YOU . . . THIS IS THE CHALICE OF MY BLOOD . . . WHICH WILL BE POURED OUT FOR YOU AND FOR MANY FOR THE FORGIVENESS OF SINS." By the power of the Holy Spirit, our gifts of bread and wine have become the very Body and Blood of the Risen Christ.

Jesus is truly present, even though the appearances of bread and wine remain. We prepare to receive Christ so that he may work in us. Together we pray the Lord's Prayer that Jesus taught us, and we pray that Christ's peace be with us always. We offer one another a sign of peace to show that we are united in Christ.

With your family, watch as the priest breaks the consecrated bread, the Body of Christ. Jesus also made this gesture—the Breaking of the Bread—at the Last Supper. It shows our unity, for in Holy Communion, we share in the one bread that is broken for us all. When we receive Holy Communion with faith and love, Christ can help us to become better, to become more patient and forgiving with a greater love and compassion for other people.

We Go in Peace . . .

In the Concluding Rites, the priest offers a final prayer and blesses us in the name of the Father, the Son, and the Holy Spirit. We hear these or other words of dismissal: "Go in peace, glorifying the Lord by your life." The Mass does not really end; it is meant to continue in our daily lives.

How will you and your family bring Christ to the world?

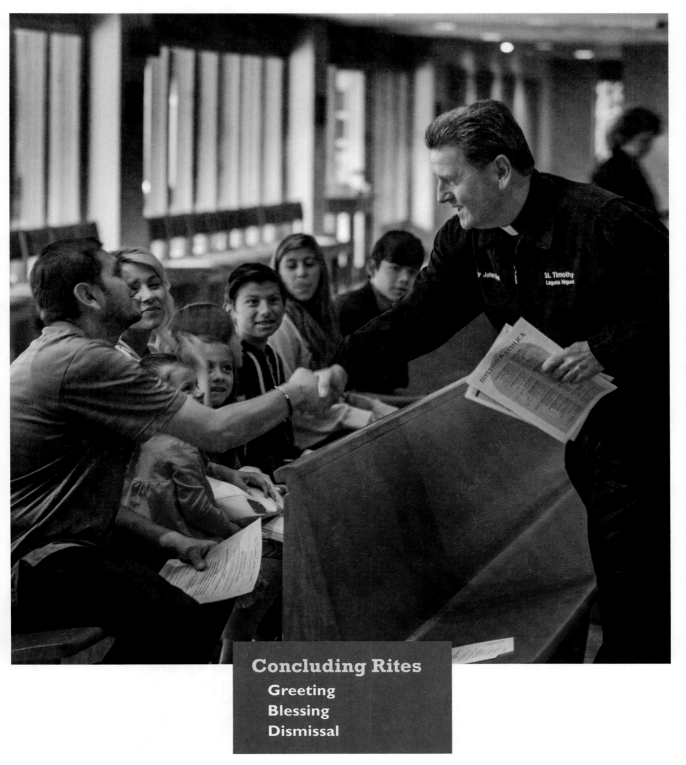

Concluding Rites
Greeting
Blessing
Dismissal

Book — 119   Luke, |10|

Chapter

Verse

Passage

Passage Title

Titles are sometimes added to show themes of the chapters, but these titles are not part of the actual words of the Bible.

Praise of the Father |21| *t u**At that very moment he rejoiced [in] the holy Spirit and said, "I give you praise, Father, Lord of heaven and earth, for although you have hidden these things from the wise and the learned you have revealed them to the childlike. Yes, Father, such has been your gracious will. 22 *v*All things have been handed over to me by my Father. No one knows who the Son is except the Father, and who the Father is except the Son and anyone to whom the Son wishes to reveal him."

A passage is a section of a chapter made up of a number of verses.

This passage shows Luke 10:21–22, which means: the Gospel of Luke, chapter ten, verses twenty-one to twenty-two.

Reading the Bible . . . in Five Easy Steps

When you are given a Scripture passage to read, here are five easy steps that will help you to find it! With your child, follow these steps to look up **Lk 10:21–22.**

1. **Find the book.** When the name of the book is abbreviated, locate the meaning of the abbreviation on the contents pages at the beginning of your Bible. *Lk* stands for Luke, one of the four Gospels.

2. **Find the page.** Your Bible's contents pages will also show the page on which the book begins. Turn to that page within your Bible.

3. **Find the chapter.** Once you arrive at the page where the book begins, keep turning the pages forward until you find the right chapter. The image above shows you how a chapter number is usually displayed on a typical Bible page. You are looking for chapter **10** in Luke.

4. **Find the verses.** Once you find the right chapter, locate the verse or verses you need within the chapter. The image above also shows you how verse numbers will look on a typical Bible page. You are looking for verses **21** and **22.**

5. **Start reading!**

Stations of the Cross

In the Stations of the Cross, we follow in the footsteps of Jesus during his Passion and Death on the Cross.

1 Jesus is condemned to die.

2 Jesus takes up his Cross.

3 Jesus falls the first time.

4 Jesus meets his mother.

5 Simon helps Jesus carry his Cross.

6 Veronica wipes the face of Jesus.

7 Jesus falls the second time.

8 Jesus meets the women of Jerusalem.

9 Jesus falls the third time.

10 Jesus is stripped of his garments.

11 Jesus is nailed to the Cross.

12 Jesus dies on the Cross.

13 Jesus is taken down from the Cross.

14 Jesus is laid in the tomb.

End each station with: We adore you, O Christ, and we bless you. Because by your holy cross you have redeemed the world.

Celebrating the Sacrament of Penance and Reconciliation

Individual confession

First, I examine my conscience.

The priest greets me.

We both make the Sign of the Cross.

The priest asks me to trust in God's mercy.

The priest or I may read from Scripture.

I talk with the priest and I confess my sins.

The priest talks to me about loving God and others.

He gives me an act of penance.

I pray an Act of Contrition.

In the name of God and the Church, the priest grants me absolution.

The priest extends his hand over my head.

I receive God's forgiveness of my sins through the words and actions of the priest.

Together, the priest and I give thanks for God's forgiveness.

I am sent to go in peace and to do the penance the priest gave me.

The Ten Commandments

1. I am the LORD your God: you shall not have strange gods before me.

2. You shall not take the name of the LORD your God in vain.

3. Remember to keep holy the LORD's Day.

4. Honor your father and your mother.

5. You shall not kill.

6. You shall not commit adultery.

7. You shall not steal.

8. You shall not bear false witness against your neighbor.

9. You shall not covet your neighbor's wife.

10. You shall not covet your neighbor's goods.

The Great Commandment

"You shall love the Lord, your God, with all your heart, with all your soul, and with all your mind. This is the greatest and the first commandment. The second is like it: You shall love your neighbor as yourself."

Matthew 22:37–39

The New Commandment

"I give you a new commandment: love one another. As I have loved you, so you also should love one another. This is how all will know that you are my disciples, if you have love for one another."

John 13:34–35

The Beatitudes

"Blessed are the poor in spirit,
for theirs is the kingdom of
heaven."

"Blessed are they who mourn,
for they will be comforted."

"Blessed are the meek,
for they will inherit the land."

"Blessed are they who hunger and
thirst for righteousness,
for they will be satisfied."

"Blessed are the merciful,"
for they will be shown mercy."

"Blessed are the clean of heart,
for they will see God."

"Blessed are the peacemakers,
for they will be called children
of God."

"Blessed are they who are persecuted
for the sake of righteousness, for
theirs in the kingdom of heaven."

Matthew 5:3–10

The Seven Sacraments

The Sacraments of Christian Initiation
Baptism
Confirmation
Eucharist

The Sacraments of Healing
Penance and Reconciliation
Anointing of the Sick

The Sacraments at the Service of Communion
Holy Orders
Matrimony

The Power of Grace

How do we live as disciples of Jesus? Through the power of God's grace, we can grow in our friendship with God. Grace is a share in God's life and love. We receive grace at our Baptism and when we receive the other sacraments. The water of Baptism is a sign of the life that God gives us through his grace. Throughout our lives, grace helps us respond to God with love. It gives us the strength to live as Jesus' disciples.

Your *Christ In Us*

Family Companion

Welcome. We are so glad that you are a ***Christ In Us*** family. In this section, you will find a treasury of resources as your family accompanies your child on our journey to a greater love in Jesus Christ. This material is written specifically for you as adult family members. But be certain that you review your child's resources that precede this section. Also, don't forget to look over the *Glossary* that follows. It will give you a good overview of what your child has been experiencing this year. Finally, the *Q&A* offers a wonderful opportunity for your entire family to review the major faith statements of the grade.

Precepts of the Church

The pope and bishops have established some laws to help us know and fulfill our responsibilities as members of the Church. These laws are called the Precepts of the Church.

It is helpful to think of the precepts as rules or principles intended as a guide for behavior. They teach us how we should act as members of the Church. These precepts also make sure that the Church has what it needs to serve its members and to grow.

1. You shall attend Mass on Sundays and Holy Days of Obligation and rest from servile labor.

2. You shall confess your sins at least once a year.

3. You shall receive the Sacrament of the Eucharist at least during the Easter season.

4. You shall observe the days of fasting and abstinence by the Church.

5. You shall help to provide for the needs of the Church.

Holy Days of Obligation

Each Sunday of the liturgical year is a great celebration of the Church, or a solemnity. In addition to each Sunday, there are other solemnities in the liturgical year on which we are obliged to attend Mass to give special honor to Jesus Christ for the salvation he has given to us. These are called Holy Days of Obligation. Post this list of holy days in your home to remind everyone of them!

- **Solemnity of Mary, Mother of God** (January 1)
- **Ascension** (when celebrated on Thursday during the Easter season*)
- **Assumption of Mary** (August 15)
- **All Saints' Day** (November 1)
- **Immaculate Conception** (December 8)
- **Christmas** (December 25)

*Some dioceses celebrate the Ascension on the following Sunday.

How to Become a Saint

Yes, it is true, everyone in your family can become a saint! Having been made holy by your Baptism and united to Christ, you are called to be a saint. Saints were ordinary human beings, just like you, who were faithful disciples of Jesus. They are followers of Christ who lived lives of holiness on earth and now share in eternal life with God in heaven. From the example of the saints' lives, we can learn ways to love God, ourselves, and others. We can learn how to be disciples of Jesus as the saints were.

Have you or your child ever wondered how the Church decides who is named a saint? Here is a brief summary of this process.

The Canonization Process

If someone who has died was known for living an especially holy life, or was martyred for his or her Catholic faith, the bishop of this person's diocese may begin the process to consider the person for sainthood.

- The first step is an investigation into the person's life. People who knew him or her are interviewed. The bishop collects information on what the person said, wrote, and did. The information is sent to the Vatican. When a person becomes a candidate for sainthood, he or she is known as "Servant of God."

- A group of cardinals at the Vatican, the Congregation for the Causes of Saints, study the information about the candidate's life. They consider whether the person is a role model for living Catholic virtues. If so, the person can be declared "Venerable."

- The next step is declaring the candidate "Blessed." This is called "beatification." Beatification occurs if it can be shown that a miracle occurred in connection with the candidate or if the person died a martyr for the faith. An example of a miracle might be a sudden cure or healing, with no reasonable medical explanation, when someone prayed for the candidate's help. The Vatican carefully reviews the evidence on any miracles.

- If a second miracle can be credited to the candidate, he or she can be named "Saint," or canonized.

Catholic Social Teaching

There are seven themes of Catholic social teaching.

Life and Dignity of the Human Person

Human life is sacred because it is a gift from God. Because we are all God's children, we all share the same human dignity. As Christians we respect all people, even those we do not know.

Call to Family, Community, and Participation

We are all social. We need to be with others to grow and learn values. As Christians, we are involved in our family life and community.

Rights and Responsibilities of the Human Person

Every person has a fundamental right to life. This includes the things we need to have a decent life: faith and family, work and education, health care and housing. We also have a responsibility to others and to society. We work to make sure the rights of all people are being protected.

Option for the Poor and Vulnerable

We have a special obligation to help those who are poor and in need. This includes those who cannot protect themselves because of their age or their health.

Dignity of Work and the Rights of Workers

Our work is a sign of our participation in God's work. People have the right to decent work, just wages, safe working conditions, and to participate in decisions about work.

Solidarity of the Human Family

Solidarity is a feeling of unity. It binds members of a group together. Each of us is a member of the one human family. The human family includes people of all racial and cultural backgrounds. We all suffer when one part of the human family suffers, whether they live near or far away.

Care for God's Creation

God created us to be stewards, or caretakers, of his creation. We must care for and respect the environment. We have to protect it for future generations. When we care for creation, we show respect for God the Creator.

A Virtuous Life

The mark of a true disciple of Christ is one who believes, hopes, and loves. The Theological Virtues—faith, hope, and love—guide the way we live. These virtues are gifts from God. At times we may have doubts or feel weak and want to give up hope. We may even act in unloving ways toward others. As a family, we participate in the sacramental life and pray together for faith, hope, and love (also called charity). The Theological and Cardinal Virtues unite us to God. Every disciple of Jesus is called to "put on" these virtues so that others can see Christ in us.

Cardinal Virtues

Prudence	helps us to use reason to find the true good in every situation.
Justice	helps us to respect other people and give them what is rightfully theirs.
Fortitude	helps us to use strength or courage to use good judgment and behavior during difficult or challenging times.
Temperance	helps us to use earthly goods in moderation.

Theological Virtues

Faith	helps us to believe in God and all that the Church teaches us; it helps us believe all that God has told us about himself and all that he has done.
Hope	helps us to trust in God's promise to share his life with us forever; it makes us confident in God's love and care for us.
Love	helps us to love God and to love our neighbor; it is the greatest of all virtues.

Practicing Devotions

Does anyone in your family practice devotions such as praying the Rosary? Devotions are a type of prayer that are not part of the liturgy of the Church but are rich and diverse expressions of faith that have been handed down to us through the centuries. Examples of devotions include novenas and the Chaplet of Divine Mercy. Devotions can draw us into the mystery of Christ among us.

Novenas

A novena is a devotion of praying for nine consecutive days. The word *novena* comes from a Latin word meaning "nine." Novenas have been prayed since the earliest days of the Church. In fact, Mary and the Apostles prayed together for a period of nine days between Jesus' Ascension and his sending of the Holy Spirit on Pentecost (see Acts of the Apostles, Chapter 1). Often people pray a novena for a special need or intention.

Chaplet of Divine Mercy

Here is one prayer you might pray with your family as a novena. The Chaplet of Divine Mercy is a devotion that is prayed using rosary beads. Saint Faustina Kowalska, who lived from 1905 to 1938 in Poland, gave this practice of praying for the mercy of Jesus Christ to the Church. The Church celebrates Divine Mercy Sunday on the Second Sunday of Easter.

1. To pray the chaplet, begin with the Sign of the Cross, an Our Father, three Hail Marys, and the Apostles' Creed, just as you would when beginning the Rosary.

2. Then, on the large bead before each decade, pray: Eternal Father, I offer you the Body and Blood, Soul and Divinity of your dearly beloved Son, Our Lord Jesus Christ, in atonement for our sins and those of the whole world.

3. On the ten small beads of each decade, pray: For the sake of his Sorrowful Passion, have mercy on us and on the whole world.

4. After five decades, pray three times: Holy God, Holy Mighty One, Holy Immortal One, have mercy on us and on the whole world.

Vocations

When we were baptized, we began our new life as Christians. Our parents and godparents wanted to share their Catholic faith with us. As we grow older, we want to grow in our Christian life as Jesus Christ teaches. Through the Church, God invites us to choose many ways of helping others. This call from God to live our Christian life more fully is our vocation.

Some vocations are celebrated as sacraments in the Church. Bishops and priests are called to lead the Catholic community in celebrating the sacraments and in teaching God's Word. Deacons are also called to serve as leaders in the Church. They are ordained ministers who help the priest serve a parish community in different ways. Deacons preach homilies and preside at the celebrations of Baptism and Matrimony.

Religious sisters and brothers dedicate their lives to serving others through the work of the Church. They may live in communities with other religious sisters and brothers. They make promises to God and their communities that they will live simply and do the work that their communities do.

The influence families have on the life of their children's vocations is essential to the life of the Church. The Christian family is the first and most important guide in this journey. Here are some ways we can promote vocations at home.

Ways to Promote Vocations

- Invite your child to identify a talent he or she has and imagine together what work or ministry God might want someone to do with that type of talent. Also talk about what good things can be done with the talent right now. For instance, singing talent could be used to sing a baby brother or sister to sleep.

- Encourage your children to be involved in the liturgical life of the parish as servers, lectors, musicians, and so on. Quiz your children and discuss with them stories of calls in Scripture (e.g., Mary's response to God in Luke 1:26–39, Jesus' calling the Apostles in Matthew 4:18–22, and so on).

- Find opportunities to affirm the gifts and talents of your children and help them relate their gifts to various careers and life choices (including priesthood and religious life).

- On the date of your child's Baptism, talk about the life of the saint for whom the child is named (or the saint's day it is). There is plenty of information about the background of saints on the Internet. The saints are people from all walks of life who tried to make a positive difference in the world—a goal as real today as it was for the saints.

- Talk positively and enthusiastically about the priests, sisters, brothers, and deacons in your parish.

Prayer for Vocations

Dear God,
You have a great and loving plan for our world and for me. I wish to share in that plan fully, faithfully, and joyfully.

Help me to understand what it is you wish me to do with my life. Help me to be attentive to the signs you give me about preparing for the future.

Help me to learn to be a sign of the kingdom, or reign, of God whether I am called to the priesthood or religious life, the single or married life.

Once I have heard and understood your call, give me the strength and the grace to follow it with generosity and love. Amen.

Glossary

anoint (page 80) to apply oil to someone as a sign that God has chosen that person for a special mission

Anointing of the Sick (page 89) the sacrament by which God's grace and comfort are given to those who are seriously ill or are suffering

Assumption (page 44) the event in which Mary, at the end of her life, was taken up by God, body and soul, into heaven

Baptism (page 79) the sacrament in which we become members of the Church and receive God's sanctifying grace and the Gift of the Holy Spirit

capital sins (page 132) the seven "deadly" sins that separate us from God and others

Cardinal Virtues (page 115) the virtues of prudence, justice, fortitude, and temperance

Chosen People (page 122) a term for the Israelites, whom God chose to be his people, and he would be their God

Church (page 52) the community of believers, led by the Holy Spirit

common priesthood of the faithful (page 94) Christ's priestly mission shared by all those who are baptized

communal prayer (page 147) prayer we pray together as a community

Communion of Saints (page 170) the whole communion of faith-filled people living now and united with those who have died but are alive with God in heaven or in Purgatory

Confirmation (page 80) the sacrament in which we are sealed with the Gift of the Holy Spirit, who strengthens us to live our baptismal promises

conscience (page 113) a God-given "interior voice" that enables us to know what is morally right or wrong

Consecration (page 82) the event at Mass in which the bread and wine truly become the Body and Blood of Christ

contemplation (page 165) a form of silent prayer in which we focus entirely on God and listen for his voice

conversion (page 136) a turning to God with all one's heart

Divine Revelation (page 20) the way God makes himself known to us

free will (page 104) God's gift of the freedom and ability to choose to cooperate with his plan for us

grace (page 52) a share in God's life

Holy Orders (page 95) the sacrament in which baptized men are ordained to serve the Church as deacons, priests, and bishops

Incarnation (page 45) the mystery of the Second Person of the Trinity, Jesus Christ, taking on a human nature

intention (page 163) the aim of our prayers or plan for them

justification (page 140) the gift by which, through Jesus' Death and Resurrection, and the grace that comes to us from it, we are forgiven of our sins and put into a right relationship with God

Kingdom of God (page 181) God's reign of peace, justice, and love

laying on of hands (page 80) a sign of God's blessing that gives authority and grace in God's name

liturgical year (page 71) the calendar that guides the liturgies and celebrations of the Church year

liturgy (page 62) the work and prayer of Christ and his Church

Liturgy of the Hours (page 157) also known as the Divine Office, the official non-sacramental, communal prayer of the Church

Liturgy of the Word (page 70) the part of the Mass in which we listen and respond to God's Word

Matrimony (page 96) the sacrament in which a baptized man and baptized woman become husband and wife and promise to be faithful to each other for the rest of their lives

meditation (page 165) a form of silent prayer that uses our thoughts, imagination, and emotions to focus on God and what he wants us to know

morality (page 105) the goodness or evil of our actions

mortal sin (page 130) very serious sin that breaks a person's friendship with God

mystery (page 20) something that is beyond our ability to understand

natural law (page 108) our God-given desire to be in right relationship with him, others, and ourselves; the moral law we are born with, placed in our hearts by God

original holiness (page 39) the original state of human beings in their relationship with God, sharing in his divine life and in full communion with him

original justice (page 39) the original state of Adam and Eve before they disobeyed God; a state of complete harmony with themselves, with each other, and with all of creation

Original Sin (page 39) the sin of the first man and woman that was passed on to all generations

particular judgment (page 40) the judgment by Jesus at the moment of our death in which he will determine how well we have followed the commandments and his teachings

Paschal Mystery (page 46) the life, Death, Resurrection, and Ascension of Jesus Christ

Penance and Reconciliation (page 86) the sacrament in which Jesus forgives our sins and heals us of both venial and mortal sin

People of God (page 52) a name for the Church and her members

prayer (page 146) raising our hearts and minds to God

Precepts of the Church (page 124) laws that help us know and fulfill our responsibilities as members of the Church and to unite us as followers of Jesus Christ

Real Presence (page 82) Jesus Christ truly present in the Eucharist, Body, Blood, Soul, and Divinity

sacramentals (page 66) blessings, actions, and objects that help us respond to God's grace received in the sacraments

sacraments (page 63) effective signs instituted by Christ and entrusted to the Church, by which divine life is shared with us

Sacraments at the Service of Communion (page 94) the Sacraments of Holy Orders and Matrimony

Sacraments of Christian Initiation (page 78) the sacraments of Baptism, Confirmation, and Eucharist, which make us members of the Church

Sacraments of Healing (page 87) the Sacraments of Penance and Reconciliation and Anointing of the Sick, the sacraments that are concerned with healing the mind, body, and soul

Sacred Chrism (page 80) oil blessed by the bishop; it is used in the Sacraments of Baptism, Confirmation, Holy Orders, and Anointing of the Sick

Sacred Scripture (page 22) holy writings in which God speaks to us in human words

Sacred Tradition (page 24) the revelation of the Good News of Jesus Christ as lived out in the Church, past and present

sanctified (page 28) made holy

sanctifying grace (page 138) the gift of God's life infused into our soul to heal us of sin and make us holy

sin (page 129) a thought, word, or deed, or a failure to do what we ought against God's law

society (page 116) a group of people bound together by a principle of unity that goes beyond any one individual, whose spiritual purpose is to fulfill the human vocation

solidarity (page 116) the Christian virtue that involves a love for all people and involves actions that work for peace, justice, and the common good

Theological Virtues (page 115) God's gifts of faith, hope, and charity that enable us to live in a relationship with the Holy Trinity

transubstantiation (page 82) the change in the substance of the bread and wine during the Consecration, though to the senses they still appear as bread and wine

venial sin (page 131) less serious sin that weakens a person's friendship with God

vice (page 132) a habit of sinful behavior

virtue (page 114) a good spiritual habit that helps us act according to God's plan for us

Q&A

Q: What is the mystery of God?

A: God is a mystery, which means that he is greater than the human mind's ability to understand. Words alone cannot fully describe who God is. *CCC, 251, 260*

Q: What is Divine Revelation?

A: Divine Revelation is God's making himself known to us. Through Divine Revelation we come to know his plan of salvation for all people. *CCC, 51, 53, 68, 69, 230*

Q: What is Sacred Scripture?

A: Sacred Scripture is God's revelation in human words. In Sacred Scripture, God speaks to his children. He lovingly meets us and talks with us in Sacred Scripture. Sacred Scripture is God's Word to us and for us. *CCC, 101, 104, 109*

Q: What is Sacred Tradition?

A: Sacred Tradition is the revelation of the Good News of Jesus Christ as lived out in the Church, past and present. *CCC, 76, 80*

Q: How can we know God?

A: We can know God through creation and the Church. When we look at God's creation with our gift of openness to truth and beauty, we can see all that God has to teach us. The Church uses the gifts of creation in her celebration of the sacraments. *CCC, 35, 47, 317*

Q: What is the Blessed Trinity?

A: The Blessed Trinity is God in Three Persons: God the Father, God the Son, and God the Holy Spirit. The Blessed Trinity is the central mystery of the Christian faith. *CCC, 253, 261*

Q: What is the soul?

A: The soul is the invisible, spiritual reality within each of us. The soul is immortal. It will never die. *CCC, 362, 363*

Q: What is faith?

A: Faith means believing that God has revealed himself to us through his words and actions, and most especially through Jesus Christ. Faith is a gift from God that guides how we live every day. The Church supports and nourishes our faith. *CCC, 1841, 1842*

Q: What is the Assumption?

A: The Assumption of the Blessed Virgin marks the event in which Mary, at the end of her life, was taken up by God, body and soul, into heaven. *CCC, 974*

CCC = Catechism of the Catholic Church

Q: What is the Paschal Mystery?

A: The Paschal Mystery is what we celebrate in the Eucharist. Specifically, it is the life, Death, Resurrection, and Ascension of Christ. *CCC, 654, 1085*

Q: What is the Incarnation?

A: The Incarnation is the mystery that Jesus became truly human while also remaining truly God. We can never totally understand its meaning. *CCC, 460, 464, 480*

Q: What is the People of God?

A: The People of God is the community of believers that make up the Church. We become members of the Church when we are baptized. Jesus Christ is the Head of the People of God and is led by the Holy Spirit. *CCC, 781, 695, 1267*

Q: What is grace?

A: Grace is God's gift of new life and friendship. The grace of Baptism puts us in a right relationship with God: it justifies us. *CCC, 1996, 1997, 2000*

Q: How is the Church divinely established?

A: The Church has a missionary mandate. This means that Jesus Christ has sent the Church out into the world to preach the Gospel to all people. *CCC, 849*

Q: What is the liturgy?

A: Liturgy is the work of Christ and his Church. Christ acts through the liturgy, particularly the sacraments, to communicate God's grace to us. *CCC, 1084, 1085*

Q: What are sacraments?

A: Sacraments are effective signs given to us by Jesus through which we share in God's life. In the sacraments, the Holy Spirit recalls the mystery of Christ. The Holy Spirit prepares our hearts and minds to encounter Jesus when we celebrate the sacraments. *CCC, 1091, 1099*

Q: How does the Church share signs of God's grace?

A: The Church's Seven Sacraments are celebrations that are special signs of God's love, presence, and saving power. Jesus instituted the sacraments. He gave them to the Church so that his saving work would continue for all time. We receive special graces from each of the sacraments when we celebrate them properly. *CCC, 1131*

Q: What are sacramentals?

A: Sacramentals are blessings, actions, and objects that help us respond to God's grace received in the sacraments. Sacramentals can help make every event in our lives holy. *CCC, 1670, 1671, 1677*

Q: What is the Liturgy of the Word?

A: The Liturgy of the Word is the part of the Mass in which we listen and respond to God's Word. *CCC, 1190*

Q: What is the liturgical year?

A: The liturgical year is the calendar that guides the liturgies and celebrations of the Church year. During the liturgical year, we recall and celebrate the whole mystery of Jesus Christ. *CCC, 1168, 1194*

Q: Why is Apostolic Tradition important?

A: Apostolic Tradition is important because it means that we celebrate one faith received from the Apostles and passed down to the Church today. This is true even when the Church's style of worship and celebrations might be different in other areas of the world. The Church all over the world celebrates the same Paschal Mystery: the Passion, Death, Resurrection, and Ascension of Jesus. *CCC, 1200–1202, 1209*

Q: What are the Sacraments of Initiation?

A: The Sacraments of Initiation are Baptism, Confirmation, and Eucharist. These sacraments of Christian initiation begin, strengthen, and nourish our life in the Church. *CCC, 1275*

Q: What is Baptism?

A: Baptism is the foundation of Christian life. It is the very first sacrament that we celebrate and leads us to the other two Sacraments of Christian Initiation, Confirmation and Eucharist. It is upon Baptism that we build our lives as followers of Christ. *CCC, 1256, 1258, 1260*

Q: What is Real Presence?

A: Real Presence is when Jesus is fully present in the Eucharist, in Body, Blood, Soul, and Divinity. When we receive Holy Communion, we are nourished by the Body and Blood of Christ. *CCC, 1410, 1413*

Q: What is Anointing of the Sick?

A: Anointing of the Sick is the sacrament by which God's grace and comfort are given to those who are seriously ill or suffering. In this sacrament, we ask God to heal us and to strengthen us to endure our suffering. *CCC, 1518, 1527, 1528*

Q: What is the common priesthood of the faithful?

A: The common priesthood of the faithful is Christ's priestly mission in which all those who are baptized share. Each of us is called to worship God, spread the Good News of Jesus Christ, and serve one another and the Church. *CCC, 1533, 1535, 1591*

Q: **What are the Sacraments at the Service of Communion?**

A: The Sacraments at the Service of Communion are the Sacraments of Holy Orders and Matrimony. Those who celebrate them help the Church grow in holiness through the ministerial priesthood and through married life. *CCC, 1534*

Q: **What is free will?**

A: Free will allows us to choose what we do. God created each of us with the gifts of intellect and free will. These gifts mean we can freely choose to cooperate with God's action in our lives and God's plan for us. *CCC, 1711, 2025*

Q: **What is morality?**

A: Morality is the goodness or evil of our actions. Every choice or act we make is based on three elements: the *objective* (what we do), the *intention* (why we do the act), and the *situation* (such as where, when, with whom, and how). *CCC, 1750–1754*

Q: **What is natural law?**

A: Natural law is an awareness of what is good and true because we are created in God's image. Natural law helps us discover, using reason, a way to true happiness. *CCC, 1955, 1956*

Q: **What is conscience?**

A: Conscience is our ability to know the difference between good and evil, between right and wrong. Educating our conscience about what is right and what is wrong is a lifelong task. *CCC, 1713, 1776, 1796*

Q: **What is virtue?**

A: A virtue is a good spiritual habit that helps us act according to God's love for us. People who are virtuous make these habits or virtues a part of their lives. *CCC, 1803, 1804, 1830*

Q: **What are the Cardinal Virtues?**

A: The moral or Cardinal Virtues are habits that come about by our own efforts. The Cardinal Virtues are the virtues of prudence, justice, fortitude, and temperance. *CCC, 1804, 1805*

Q: **What is the New Law?**

A: The New Law, or Law of Love, is the work of Christ. In the Sermon on the Mount, Christ taught us a way of living, a law of love for God, self, and neighbor. It shows us the way to achieve eternal life. *CCC, 1949, 1950, 1965, 1966, 1983*

Q: What are the Ten Commandments?

A: The Ten Commandments strengthen our relationship with God. God's purpose in giving us the commandments was to teach us how to live in right relationship with him. God gives us the grace we need to follow his commandments. *CCC, 2082, 2085*

Q: What are the Precepts of the Church?

A: The Precepts of the Church are positive laws that present the minimum of what a Catholic should do in order to grow in love of God and neighbor. These laws remind us that we are called to grow in holiness and serve the Church. *CCC, 2041, 2042, 2043*

Q: What is Original Sin?

A: Original Sin is the first sin, which happened when the first man and woman, Adam and Eve, disobeyed God. Baptism frees us from Original Sin. *CCC, 1707, 1714*

Q: What is sin?

A: Sin is an offense against God. When we sin, we turn our hearts away from God's love and choose that which we know is wrong. The choices we make weaken God's life in us. Sin is a thought, word, deed, or a failure to do what we ought against God's law. *CCC, 1871, 1872*

Q: What is venial sin?

A: Venial sin is less serious sin that weakens our friendship with God. Even though venial sins do not turn us completely away from God, they still harm our relationship with him, others, and the Church. *CCC, 1855, 1863*

Q: What is communal prayer?

A: Communal prayer is prayer we pray together as a community. It helps us to become aware and remember God's presence. *CCC, 2566, 2567, 2591*

Q: What is contemplation?

A: Contemplation is silent prayer in which we focus entirely on God and his presence in us. In contemplative prayer, our mind is quieter and we simply sit in the presence of God and listen for his voice. *CCC, 2705, 2708, 2721*

Q: What is the Communion of Saints?

A: The Communion of Saints is the whole community of faith-filled people living now united with those who have died but are alive with God in heaven or in Purgatory. To profess that we are a part of the Communion of Saints is to say that we are connected to all faithful people living and who have died. *CCC, 960, 1055*

Q: **What are the liturgical seasons?**

A: Liturgical seasons are the seasons in the calendar year that celebrate special people and events in our Church. They are Advent, Christmas, Ordinary Time, Lent, the Triduum, and Easter. *CCC, 1158–1173*

Q: **Why do we celebrate Advent?**

A: Advent is the time of year when we remember and celebrate the fact that Jesus Christ will come again in glory. No one knows the day or the hour when Christ will return. Therefore, we must be ready to meet him whenever he comes, our hearts filled with wonder, love, and praise. *CCC, 524*

Q: **Why do we celebrate Christmas?**

A: We celebrate Christmas because it is the feast of the Incarnation: Jesus, the Son of God, was born like us in all things but sin. The Word was made flesh. The Incarnation strengthens Catholics in the belief that God works through the material world rather than remaining far apart from it. *CCC, 525, 526, 1171*

Q: **Why do we celebrate Lent?**

A: Lent is a season in which we renew our faith. Just as Jesus went out into the desert and fasted for forty days to prepare for his mission, so we renew our commitment each year during the forty days of Lent. *CCC, 1438*

Q: **What is the Triduum?**

A: The Triduum is the high point of the whole Church year. It is three especially holy days in which we recall the Last Supper, the Passion and Death of Jesus on the Cross, and God raising Jesus from the dead. *CCC, 1168*

Q: **Why do we celebrate Easter?**

A: We celebrate Easter because it is the season in the liturgical year in which we remember the Resurrection of Jesus Christ and renew our life in Christ. *CCC, 1169*

Q: **What is Pentecost?**

A: Pentecost is the day the Church celebrates the descent of the Holy Spirit on the disciples of Jesus after his Ascension. It is held on the seventh Sunday after Easter. The Church celebrates the way in which the Holy Spirit fulfills the promises of Jesus and showers gifts on us. *CCC, 696, 715, 731*

Q: **What is Ordinary Time?**

A: The season of Ordinary Time is a time for the Church to reflect on Christ's life and to grow in faithfulness to his teachings. *CCC, 495, 508*

Index